ANGEL ASTROLOGY
101

"I'd Change My Life If I Had More Time"
Divine Guidance
Chakra Clearing
Angel Therapy®
The Lightworker's Way
Constant Craving A–Z
Constant Craving
The Yo-Yo Diet Syndrome
Losing Your Pounds of Pain

Audio/CD Programs

The Healing Miracles of Archangel Raphael
Angel Therapy® Meditations
Archangels 101 (abridged audio book)
Fairies 101 (abridged audio book)
Goddesses & Angels (abridged audio book)
Angel Medicine (available as both 1- and 2-CD sets)
Angels among Us (with Michael Toms)
Messages from Your Angels (abridged audio book)
Past-Life Regression with the Angels
Divine Prescriptions
The Romance Angels
Connecting with Your Angels
Manifesting with the Angels
Karma Releasing
Healing Your Appetite, Healing Your Life
Healing with the Angels
Divine Guidance
Chakra Clearing

DVD Program

How to Give an Angel Card Reading

Oracle Cards (divination cards and guidebook)

Earth Angels Tarot Cards
(with Radleigh Valentine; available December 2014)
Past Life Oracle Cards (with Brian Weiss, M.D.; available October 2014)
Cherub Angel Cards for Children (available June 2014)
Angels of Abundance Tarot Cards (with Radleigh Valentine)
Talking to Heaven Mediumship Cards (with James Van Praagh)
Archangel Power Tarot Cards (with Radleigh Valentine)
Flower Therapy Oracle Cards (with Robert Reeves)
Indigo Angel Oracle Cards (with Charles Virtue)
Angel Dreams Oracle Cards (with Melissa Virtue)
Mary, Queen of Angels Oracle Cards
Angel Tarot Cards (with Radleigh Valentine and Steve A. Roberts)
The Romance Angels Oracle Cards
Life Purpose Oracle Cards
Archangel Raphael Healing Oracle Cards
Archangel Michael Oracle Cards
Angel Therapy® Oracle Cards

Magical Messages from the Fairies Oracle Cards
Ascended Masters Oracle Cards
Daily Guidance from Your Angels Oracle Cards
Saints & Angels Oracle Cards
Magical Unicorns Oracle Cards
Goddess Guidance Oracle Cards
Archangel Oracle Cards
Magical Mermaids and Dolphins Oracle Cards
Messages from Your Angels Oracle Cards
Healing with the Fairies Oracle Cards
Healing with the Angels Oracle Cards

All of the above are available at your local bookstore, or may be ordered by visiting: Hay House USA: www.hayhouse.com®; Hay House Australia: www .hayhouse.com.au; Hay House UK: www.hayhouse.co.uk; Hay House South Africa: www.hayhouse.co.za; Hay House India: www.hayhouseco.in

Doreen's website: www.AngelTherapy.com

✳

ALSO BY YASMIN BOLAND

Books

Carole King is an Alien (Penguin)
All the Rage (Penguin)
Horoscope Year Ahead Series – 2005 (New Holland)
Horoscope Year Ahead Series – 2004 (New Holland)
Cosmic Love (Penguin)

Yasmin's website: www.yasminboland.com

ANGEL ASTROLOGY

101

DISCOVER THE ANGELS CONNECTED WITH YOUR BIRTH CHART

DOREEN VIRTUE
AND YASMIN BOLAND

HAY HOUSE, INC.
Carlsbad, California * New York City
London * Sydney * Johannesburg
Vancouver * Hong Kong * New Delhi

Published and distributed in the United States by: Hay House, Inc.: www.hayhouse
.com® • *Published and distributed in Australia by:* Hay House Australia Pty. Ltd.: www
.hayhouse.com.au • *Published and distributed in the United Kingdom by:* Hay House
UK, Ltd.: www.hayhouse.co.uk • *Published and distributed in the Republic of South
Africa by:* Hay House SA (Pty), Ltd.: www.hayhouse.co.za • *Distributed in Canada by:*
Raincoast Books: www.raincoast.com • *Published in India by:* Hay House Publishers
India: www.hayhouse.co.in

Cover and interior design: Tricia Breidenthal
Cover artwork: Jeffrey K. Bedrick

Library of Congress Cataloging-in-Publication Data

Virtue, Doreen.
  Angel astrology 101 : discover the angels connected with your birth chart / Doreen
Virtue and Yasmin Boland. -- 1st edition.
     pages cm
  ISBN 978-1-4019-4305-9 (hardcover : alk. paper) 1. Zodiac. 2. Angels. 3. Astrology.
I. Title.
  BF1726.V56 2014
  133.5'2--dc23

                              2013019329

Hardcover ISBN: 978-1-4019-4305-9

17 16 15 14   4 3 2 1
1st edition, March 2014

Printed in China

CONTENTS

INTRODUCTION

ANGELS AND ASTROLOGY

Astrology is an ancient predictive and healing practice based upon our ancestors' observations of the movement of the Sun, Moon, planets, and stars. A bit like Tarot cards, the exact history of how astrology developed remains mysterious. There are great chunks missing from the timeline of its evolution (modern-day astrologers are trying to unearth this missing information).

What many historians suspect is that astrology first came into being as a direct result of ancient humans' need to work with the seasons. Long before the advent of organized agriculture, men and women required information on when the seasons would change. They wanted to know when it would be hot or cold, what the tides were doing, when certain plants were more likely to blossom, and so on. They had to be able to predict, at least to some extent, what was going to happen. They soon realized that they could use the repetitive cycles of the Sun and Moon to reliably work out a lot of this information in advance.

Archaeologists have discovered cave markings showing that lunar cycles (for example, when the Moon is full or new) were being noted as far back as 25,000 years ago. Of course, back then, people lived mostly outdoors and were entirely connected to nature, so it was natural that they tuned in to these cycles.

So, first our ancestors worked out how to predict the movements of the Sun, the Moon, and their relation to the stars. Next came the discovery of the planets in our solar system. The inner planets, Mercury and Venus; and the outer planets, Mars, Jupiter, and Saturn, are visible to the naked eye. They were all identified by ancient Babylonian astronomers around the 2nd millennium B.C. Uranus, Neptune, and Pluto were discovered after the telescope was invented in 1608.

Initially, our ancestors noticed patterns between what happened when the Moon disappeared (at the

time of the New Moon) versus what happened when the Moon swelled to roundness (when full). Later, stargazers began to note correlations between the movements of the planets and life here on Earth. Put very simply, they plotted the angles that the planets made as they went around the sun. Then they observed what was happening down here on Earth at that time. Astrologers started to classify some angles as *easy* and others as *clashing*. Imagine that some angles sound like beautiful music, while some sound like discordant clashes. Understanding this music of the spheres is the job of the astrologer.

The presumed Father of Astrology was a man named Hermes Trismegistus, whom Doreen wrote about in her book *Angel Medicine*. Doreen's research showed that Hermes was a great teacher and leader in Atlantis, and then in Egypt, following the great Flood. He is said to be the grandson of the first man, Adam, and is also credited with the expression "As above, so below," which he inscribed on the famous Emerald Tablet as part of his Hermetic teachings. The phrase means: *What happens up in the Heavens is reflected down here on Earth.* If you bear in mind Trismegistus's assertion that "we are all connected to all life everywhere," it's not such a big leap to think that we're also connected to the planets.

*

Ancient Babylonians, Egyptians, Indians, Arabians, and Greeks, as well as Kabbalists in the Judaic tradition, all had input into the development of astrology as we know it now. Along the way, our ancestors noticed patterns among the dispositions of people according to their time, date, and place of birth. These observations also became the basis for modern natal astrology.

While astrology isn't a true science, there are ancient truisms that lend it validity. As you will see throughout this book, each sign has its strengths and its shadow side. Your strengths are to be used to help others, and your shadow side is something for you to work on healing.

Initially, it was rare that anyone except kings and queens knew the day of their birth, let alone the hour. So ancient astrology had little to do with what we think of as astrology today. Ordinary people didn't get their charts read. Only *ye olde* kings would have a court astrologer note when certain planets were getting together in harmonious or angry ways. They informed their king of the best times to shore up relations with an ally or launch an attack against an enemy, for example.

Modern-Day Astrology

Today, if you consult an astrologer, you will be asked the time, date, and place of your birth. Based on this information, the astrologer will note where the planets were on the day you were born. This person will also know whether the planets were making beautiful music together or clashing. This is called *natal astrology.*

It may be that until now, all you've known about astrology is what you've read in newspapers and magazines. This is called *solar astrology,* as it simply looks at your Sun, which represents your ego. This type of astrology is very much a "quick fix," compared to having your entire chart examined. Even so, there's nothing inherently wrong with it.

Columns in newspapers and magazines are often the first initiation into astrology for many people. This type of astrology is very accessible and can be an excellent vehicle for Divine messages from the cosmos. In fact, newspaper or media astrology got a bad rap because in the 20th century, these columns were often written by the office intern who also made the coffee! They had nothing at all to do with real astrology. Times have changed, though, and today the majority of columns published in the media have qualified astrologers behind them.

Spiritual Astrology

It's obviously not just kings, queens, and presidents who can benefit from astrology. Astrology is a trustworthy pathway to self-discovery for all. Through astrology, you can understand your personality, relationships, moods, energy cycles, and even your life purpose. Astrology is aligned with all religious and spiritual paths, as it's a time-honored tradition for unlocking your Book of Life.

Some Christians have been raised to fear astrology, and we completely respect everyone's religious beliefs. It's interesting to note that many believe that the Three Wise Men in the Bible were actually astrologers themselves! They were, of course, following the Star of Bethlehem. In 1600, Johannes Kepler, a key figure in the 17th-century scientific revolution, hypothesized that this star was actually a conjunction of Jupiter and Saturn. It is postulated that these three astrologers were guided by God to honor Jesus's birth.

In ancient Babylon, it was common for the study of celestial movements (astronomy) to be combined with professions such as medicine, the priesthood, and teaching. Moreover, although some in the church now take a dim view of astrology, many ancient synagogues and churches feature magnificent ceiling and floor mosaics and designs depicting the 12 signs of the zodiac. For example, there is San Miniato in Florence, Italy, the most famous astrology church in Europe. This beautiful basilica and its 13th-century astrological floor feature a stunning mix of astrological and Christian symbolism, as was commonplace in medieval times before the church seemingly changed its mind about the ancient practice of astrology, which honors the heavens and the seasons.

There's even some reason to believe that Jesus himself may have been trained in astrology. One of the roles of Chaldean priests at the time of Christ's birth was to find children born under significant astrological alignments, such as the Jupiter/Saturn Star of Bethlehem. The magi would leave gifts with the parents to help pay for the raising of the children, and then seek out the brightest of these young ones for a Chaldean education once they were old enough.

If you're familiar with the Bible, you know that there's a significant period of Jesus's life—from birth to about 18 years old—which isn't accounted for. Some believe that during this time, Jesus was receiving the best education that his era had to offer: magi training, which included getting a working knowledge of astrology, as well as the healing arts. Many believe that Jesus was the greatest healer to have ever lived, but was he also an astrologer?

In his book *The Secret Zodiac,* author Fred Gettings writes: "The true books of the esoteric astrology of the mediaeval era are not to be found in manuscripts, but in stone and marble of the mediaeval cathedrals and churches."

Many astrologers who believe God intended human beings to decode the Heavens for clues point to the passage in the Bible (Luke 21:25) where it is written that "there will be signs in sun and moon and stars."

Then there is the passage from the actual Creation story itself in Genesis, which seems to suggest that humans were instructed by God to look to the heavens for signs:

> And God said, "Let there be lights in the firmament of the heavens to separate the day from the night; and *let them be for signs*

and for seasons and for days and years, and let them be lights in the firmament of the heavens to give light upon the earth." And it was so. And God made the two great lights, the greater light to rule the day, and the lesser light to rule the night; he made the stars also. (Genesis 1:14–16 RSV; emphasis added).

Yasmin says: "On a personal note, before I decided to commit my professional life to astrology, I meditated and prayed about it long and hard. Being raised a Catholic, I was aware that many in the church feared astrology. I didn't even dare tell my grandmother that I had taken up the study of it. Reading up on astrology's history, I became convinced that astrology had been sanctioned by the church for millennia until all of a sudden it was cast out. I asked Jesus for a clear sign about whether or not I should pursue astrology as a career path. Just one or two days after praying about this, I was asked to write a very high-profile and lucrative horoscope column. I took this as a sign that I was being supported by the Heavens in my pursuit of an astrological career!"

Astrology and Angels

Just as everyone has an astrological birth chart, so do we all have assigned guardian angels. These are personal angels who are with you prior to birth, all throughout your life, and in Heaven after your physical passing. Guardian angels aren't departed relatives; they are egoless celestial beings who are enacting God's will of peace through everyone.

Your guardian angels provide you with continuous love, support, and guidance. They also do their best to protect you, provided that you notice and follow their guidance in the form of warning thoughts, gut feelings, and signs.

In addition to personal guardian angels, the archangels also provide guidance and protection. Archangels are large, powerful angels who oversee guardian angels. Each archangel has a specialty. For example, Archangel Michael offers protection and courage, Raphael administers healing, Gabriel provides nurturing and messages, Uriel shines light, and so forth.

All of Heaven respects the free will of humans, so angels and archangels will never push their guidance upon you. Rather, they will wait until you pray to God for help, or ask for assistance. Only then are angels and archangels allowed to intervene.

Fortunately, it doesn't matter *how* you ask for Heavenly help—whether through formal prayer, affirmations, a fervent plea, a letter, or visualization. What matters is that you *do* ask for help.

Archangels are larger and more powerful than guardian angels. Many people are familiar with the iconic four archangels: Michael, Raphael, Gabriel, and Uriel. In addition, there are hundreds of other famous and not-so-famous archangels who are trustworthy and benevolent messengers of God. In this book, we will work with 12 sacred archangels whom I (Doreen) have carefully studied and connected with.

Each archangel's specialty corresponds with the traits associated with each astrological sign. That doesn't mean that these archangels only work with that particular astrological sign, though. The archangels are unlimited beings who work with everyone who calls upon them.

Since the archangels have specific roles and traits, they are a paired match with each astrological sign. In this book, we've detailed how to gain more understanding about yourself and more overall life satisfaction by connecting with the archangels who are specific to your astrological chart.

We've devoted each chapter to one of the 12 astrological signs, and there's an archangel associated with each sign. In addition, we've subdivided each chapter to include Sun, Moon, Mercury, Venus, Mars, and Rising (Ascendant) signs. Read each section that relates to your chart to know which archangel works with you and your sign. Ultimately, you'll read about three specific archangels, one each for your Sun, Moon, Mercury, Venus, Mars, and Rising signs.

Defining Our Terms

If you're a beginner to astrology, you may find the jargon initially confusing. But hang in there, because it will all make sense if you keep studying and pondering this material. Basically, when we talk about your "Birth Chart," we're referring to the positions in Heaven corresponding to the moment you were born.

As you may know, *astronomy* (the scientific study of stars and planets) uses the ancient "constellation" system. Our ancestors didn't have television, and they spent a lot of time outdoors. As they gazed at the sky, they saw shapes formed from the outlines of stars and planets. It was like a giant dot-to-dot drawing.

They projected their cultural and religious stories onto the canvas of the nighttime sky. So, the constellations have names according to the shapes they noticed, and the stories they told about these shapes. As the earth moves through the seasons, these shapes overhead bring the same patterns into our modern skies that our ancestors studied and taught.

So if, for example, the Sun was moving through the constellation of Leo the Lion when you were born, then your Sun sign would be Leo. The zodiac belt is a depiction of images and archetypes associated with the constellations.

Your Sun

Your Sun sign is dictated by which constellation the Sun was in on the day you were born. You might call this your Star sign. Astrologers call it your *Sun sign.* Your Sun is the essential you—the core you. In many ways it's the most important part of your chart. The Sun is very yang, so it's a more male energy in your chart, even if you are female (the Moon is the feminine energy). The Sun is all about will, power, and desire (but not usually in a sexual way). The sign your Sun is in colors how you express that will

Important note for Cusp babies: If you were born on the cusp of a sign (the day when the Sun moves from one sign to the next), you are not "a bit of both signs." You are one or the other—it's that simple. Many people don't realize that the Sun doesn't actually move from one sign into the next on the exact same day each year. There's a variation of up to three days. The dates that you read in horoscopes in magazines and newspapers (and also in this book!) are actually an arbitrary guide. That's why they can vary from one publication to another. For example, someone born on November 22 one year could be a Sagittarius, while someone born on November 22 another year could be a Scorpio. Please feel free to use our chart generator at www.moonology.com/angelcharts to find out your Sun sign, once and for all.

Your Moon

Your *Moon sign* is dictated by which sign the Moon was in at the time of your birth. The Moon spends about two and a half days in each sign, so even if you don't know your *exact* time of birth, it's often still possible to work out your Moon sign. Your Moon is another of the main centers of interest in your chart. It tells an astrologer a lot about you: what you need, how you feel, and what you're like emotionally—for example, stable or spontaneous, cautious or calculating. It also represents the most important women in your life (your mother, wife, sister, and so on). Plus, it has to do with what makes you feel comfortable—like the way you felt when your mother cared for you (hopefully).

Your Mercury

Mercury is all about how you express your-self—the way you talk, write, and think. Mercury influences how you make decisions and whether you're outspoken or quiet. It even influences which books you read, write, or enjoy. It's about words, language, where your ideas come from, where your attention is, and how well you communicate your thoughts. It's about how you learn and how your brain works, and it determines if you're likely to jump to conclusions or make considered responses. It's about whether you're stubborn, curious, or prefer to not analyze things.

Your Venus

Venus in your chart is about how you love, whom you love, and what you love. It's about relating to others. Venus also shows what kind of romantic partner and friends you seek and how you attract people. The sign and state of your Venus guides whether you're the detached or clingy type, or someone who needs a gorgeous lover, as well as whether you have high or low standards for partnership, or are someone who is worried there's not enough love to go around. Venus is also about aesthetic tastes and how you express yourself creatively. Venus guides other things, like beauty, pleasure, and abundance, but for this book we're focusing mostly on love relationships.

Your Mars

Mars is the planet of anger, aggression, sexual intimacy, and determination. The sign and state of your Mars will describe how you chase after people, dreams, jobs, and anything else. Mars is the planet that you use when you argue or fight. It determines your conflict-resolution style: whether you're likely to fly into a rage or your temper has a slow burn, whether you're a peaceful negotiator or you're conflict phobic. Because Mars is also all about sexual intimacy, it speaks volumes about whether you're an earthy lover, insecure, sensual, or romantic. Your Mars guides how you get things done and what motivates you.

Your Ascendant (or Rising) Sign

Your *Ascendant* (also known as your *Rising*) *sign* is dictated by your time, date, and place of birth. It's a record of the constellation that was coming up over the eastern horizon at the time of your birth, as seen from the place you were born. You really do need to know your time of birth pretty precisely (say within 15 minutes) to get any kind of accuracy with this.

✳

To find out your Sun, Moon, and Rising sign, there are many computer programs, apps, and sites where you can access your natal-chart information. Just go to any major search engine and plug in the keywords "Free Natal Chart" or "Free Astrology Chart," and you'll find them. You shouldn't have to buy anything or provide your e-mail address on reputable sites, which will have built-in computer programs to instantly generate charts. If you don't have access to a computer or the Internet, a local astrologer in your area will be able to work out your natal chart for a fee.

The information you'll need for your chart is:

- Your date of birth

- Your time of birth

- Your place of birth

If you don't know your time of birth, ask your parents or check your birth certificate. Many hospitals around the world keep a record of birth times. The more accurate you are with respect to your birth time, the better—ideally within about 15 minutes maximum.

Birth Details

If you're unclear about your birth details (for example, if you were adopted and don't have access to your records), you can consult an astrologer who will help do what's called a "rectification" on your chart. This method is like using astrology backward: by plotting out your major life events (for example, when you were born, when you married, had children, or maybe were divorced), an astrologer can come close to finding your correct time, date, and place of birth. Of course, most people know their date and place of birth, but this method also works for those who are unsure about their time of birth.

Another method to find out your birth data is to see a kinesiologist. Kinesiologists believe that all memory is stored in the body. Their muscle-testing techniques can help your body remember your birth time—or at least, that's the theory! To find a kinesiologist, go online or ask for help at your local mind-body-spirit bookstore.

Please don't feel bad if you don't know your time of birth. You can also wing it a little (at least to start with). Use 6 A.M. as your birth time, and pay no attention to the sections about your Rising sign. There's a chance you'll end up with the wrong Moon sign.

If your Moon-sign reading in this book doesn't resonate at all, check the reading for the Moon sign before and after the one the computer came up with. You should recognize yourself in there, one way or another. If your interest in understanding your chart deepens, you can use the methods mentioned

previously (checking records, rectification, kinesiology, and so on) to expand your exploration.

Ultimately . . .

Even if you can't get your natal chart done right away, you can still benefit from this book by reading about your Sun sign and your connection to the archangels. You can instantly know your Sun sign by looking at the birth dates for each sign, provided at the beginning of each chapter.

* * *

You can call upon Archangel Ariel for any of the following, no matter what your sign is:

1. If life feels stagnant and you need a breath of fresh air

2. When you want to spend more time in nature but can't find the time

3. If you want to help create a beautiful garden outside your home

4. If you want to create a small herb garden or indoor plant arrangement

5. When you feel as though you have lost your youthful spark

6. If you need help getting started on a project

7. When you are generally lacking in motivation to keep on going

8. When you want to start a relationship or situation all over again

9. If you need to forgive, forget, and move on

10. When you need a makeover

11. When there is something you want to manifest

12. If you need help dealing with anger issues or fear that you're acting selfishly

13. If you want to adopt a pet

14. If you sense you're addicted to your computer or cell phone

15. When you're in a hurry and running behind schedule

16. If you need to break through a fear in order to live life more fully

17. If you need to get back into your exercise routines

18. When life is lacking in spontaneity

19. When you need to stay on track

20. When you want to connect with the fairies and other elementals.

CHAPTER ONE

ARIES AND ARCHANGEL ARIEL

* * * * * * * * * * * * * * * * *

March 21–April 20

As you may know, there are 12 astrological signs. Aries is the first, and appears at the start of the astrological wheel. Therefore, this sign is known as the "child" of the astrological cycle and is associated with the season of spring, where everything is new again.

How perfect, then, that Archangel Ariel—the nature angel associated with the fairies and the elementals—is the Aries archangel. It's a perfect energetic fit!

Archangel Ariel's wonderful clean energy is sprightly. Ariel is strongly associated with baby animals and the outdoors, so you may feel an affinity with both of those parts of life if Aries is strong in your chart (that is, if your Sun, Moon, or Rising sign is in Aries).

But no matter where you have Aries in your chart, remember this: Aries is a sign that exudes innocence (like that of a child). Wherever you have Aries in your chart is the life area where you can stay forever young. Also, wherever you have Aries in your chart is where you're spontaneous and willing to go "where angels fear to tread." Hopefully, now that you're reading this book, you'll realize that there's no place angels won't go if you need them to be by your side!

So that you can get a better idea of how the Aries/Ariel energy works together, think a little more about spring. Whether you live in the Northern or the Southern Hemisphere, spring is a time of renewal and hope. Buds appear and then bloom, and the world is full of promise after a long, cold winter. The

slate is clean. A walk in nature at this time can lift your spirits sky-high.

Archangel Ariel and Aries encourage you to take off the winter layers and get back out into the natural world. Wherever you have these energies in your chart is where you're able to slough off the past and breathe in freshness. If you have a strong Aries energy in your chart (that is, if your Sun, Moon, or Rising sign is Aries), you're like a breath of fresh air to people. That's why those with a lot of Aries energy tend to be rather popular (as long as they don't let their fiery tempers get the best of them).

Archangel Ariel is also known as the "Angelic Ambassador of Divine Magic and Miraculous Manifestation." She reminds you that anything is possible if you approach life with the innocence of a child. Doing so can work wonders! If you have Aries and Ariel strong in your chart, you're going to be the person who reminds your friends and family that they really can do whatever they put their minds to, no matter what has happened in the past. You can tell them, "There's no reason to give up, even if life seems to be presenting problems!"

Archangel Ariel can help with relationships, because one of her most wonderful qualities is her dedication to helping us shake off the illusion that we're all separate beings. And she's right! *We are all connected.* Ariel can teach all of us this important lesson.

However, if Aries/Ariel is strong in your natal chart, perhaps you've already realized that we're all in this life together. Remind yourself of this fact if you feel that famous Aries "Me, me, me!" energy rising. Aries is renowned for being a self-centered sign at times. Just like the adorable children who are still under the illusion that they're the center of the Universe, Aries individuals can sometimes act like they're the only ones who matter. It's a part of their lovely naïveté, but it can upset people.

Anytime you feel your Aries energy or your ego taking over, call upon Archangel Ariel for help. She will remind you that we're all one, and that any feelings of separateness come from the ego and are pure illusion. Aries is ruled by fiery Mars and can be rather—shall we say—assertive. This also applies if you feel yourself becoming overly competitive with friends and colleagues. Competition is healthy, but don't let it hurt your relationships or lead you down a path lacking compassion.

All of the astrological signs have issues to deal with. We incarnate as a particular sign so we can face them. The good news is that there's also magic inherent in Aries that comes from this same will-ful spirit. For example, Aries is about enthusiasm and taking on adventures. Archangel Ariel will join you when you dare to step out into the world. She's happy to go on magical journeys with you, where you delight in the great outdoors, breathe in clean air, and remember who you really are. It's all a mat-ter of stepping away from the computer, the televi-sion, and electricity. Being outside is a very quick way to connect with Archangel Ariel's energy when you need to. Look at where Aries is in your chart, and see if you're being adventurous in this part of your life.

Another wonderful Aries characteristic is that this sign is relatively fearless. Meanwhile, Archangel Ariel is very adept at helping us manifest. What a powerful combination of fearless manifestation this brings about!

When we lose our fear, we step into a whole new arena of life, one where we can work with the Creator to bring about the life of our dreams. Aries is about starting over, and what could be better than starting over minus the fears that have held us back? Ariel can take us out of our comfort zones so that we can try new things. Aries supports being bold and brave and not overthinking.

Once again, look at where Aries is in your chart, and check to see if there are fears in this part of your life that can be released. Ask Archangel Ariel to help you manifest sparkling new developments. Aries is about the new, and Ariel can help you release the old so that the new can blossom. These two energies work so well together to help you remember that life is like a garden and grows what you choose to plant in it.

Do remember that Aries and Archangel Ariel are about treading lightly upon the earth. The key words for their energy are *freshness* and *vitality*. One of the worst things an Aries can do is clog up his or her system with negativity. That's why Archangel Ariel wants you to get outside and also keep your body very healthy with fresh produce. Above all, no matter what your sign, keep away from drugs and alcohol if you want to work with these energies. They will do nothing but slow down your system and act as a sort of glue that stops your wheels from turning.

Sun in Aries

If your Sun is in Aries, your core energy is touched with the vitality of Ariel, and you have her sprightly energy—what a blessing! You're a breath of fresh air for others when you walk into a room. Like Ariel, you don't take life too seriously, and you can bring a light touch to any situation.

Your sign, Aries, is about freshness, and Archangel Ariel helps you exude this energy. If you ever feel as though you've lost your spark, appeal to Ariel, who will willingly help you overcome this negativity.

Please also remember that impulsiveness is an Aries trait, so do ask Ariel for help when you know you're racing so fast that you're getting ahead of yourself. Learning to slow down is one of your life lessons. It's the angels' sacred honor to help you center yourself in peace.

One thing you may not yet have realized is that you're a great manifester, thanks to Ariel's strong presence in your birth chart. The next time you really want something to come into your life, visualize it, draw it, write down your goals, and ask Ariel for help.

You are a Divine being, and a part of this makeup is Ariel, an expert manifester. Ariel is a strong force in your life because your Aries Sun is also a major force in your life. You are more magical than you probably realize, and you inspire others with the way you take on life so boldly—with adventure always at the forefront of your mind.

Just remember that life does go in cycles, so on those occasions when you feel that your magnificent Aries spark is burning dimly, you can ask Ariel to help you regain your magic. Ariel is always there for you!

Moon in Aries

If your Moon is in Aries, you may be emotionally impulsive, as your Moon is in the fire sign of Aries and is guided by Archangel Ariel, who loves to speed through life with the next adventure in mind. Of course you race along emotionally!

The Moon governs what you need, so having Aries/Ariel here is a clear indicator that you need to fly through life fast and furiously, without having too many people reminding you of your responsibilities. There will be other facets in your chart that are about taking things slowly and seriously. You have to allow your true nature to shine, and part of that nature is that you—like Ariel—are about actively seeking fun. (You need fun the way everyone else needs food.) Thankfully, Archangel Ariel understands that and will always be with you, helping you fulfill your emotional need to laugh and to make others do so as well.

Just remember the angelic law, though: you have to *ask* for help before your angels can help you. When life feels like it's getting too staid or difficult, ask Ariel to help you recover your magical mojo. Life is what you make it, and you know that, thanks to your magical Aries Moon, blessed with the mischievous Ariel energy.

A little reminder for you that could serve you well: if you do get down in the dumps, a walk in nature could be just what you need to revive your spirits. (Ask Ariel to accompany you!)

Mercury in Aries

Aries is a very speedy sign and quick on the draw, and Mercury is the planet of communications. Put them together and you can sometimes end up with someone who is brave enough to speak his or her truth but without always considering the impact these words will have on the person he or she is talking to! If you have Mercury in Aries, you need to watch out that you don't speak too soon—all of the time!

Luckily you have Archangel Ariel, the angel that treads lightly upon the earth, guiding your Mercury in Aries. If you know you have a tendency to "shoot from the lip," call upon Archangel Ariel before going into any important meetings. Ask for help with staying quiet, and not interrupting!

Archangel Ariel knows how to start things over, too. Remember, she is about the springtime, when nature begins again. So anytime you have overstepped the mark with someone, be it at work or in your personal life, you can ask Archangel Ariel to help you find the words you need to make things right. If and when you feel yourself starting to talk heatedly, remember to ask Archangel Ariel to bring you back into line!

Aries and Archangel Ariel

Aries and Mercury are both very action-oriented, so you should find you are great at getting going with new projects. However, if you find it hard to finish those projects (sound familiar?), ask Archangel Ariel to help you keep the Aries flame burning so you see things through to completion.

Overall, this placement is a huge blessing and can boost your creativity. It also means you breathe fresh air into any conversation. You don't get bogged down in details—far from it, in fact. Instead, you have the ability to check off all the topics on anyone's list and then move on. If all committees had at least one Aries Mercury member, things would move a lot faster!

Venus in Aries

Having Venus in Aries is a huge blessing but also carries a great deal of responsibility. Venus is the planet of love and abundance. Aries is a feisty, spontaneous, and very youthful sign. When they are combined like this, you get someone who is capable of loving like he or she has never been hurt.

This is a great advantage, of course. Compared with those who hang on to past hurts and wrongs, your ability to love afresh and anew in every relationship seems like a heavenly gift. And you can see how this ties in with "spring has sprung"! Your Venus in Aries is like Ariel's springtime blossoms. Your love makes others forget about the long, cold winter they have just come through!

Do bear in mind that not everyone has your ability to kiss and make up and move on. Not everyone can make such swift decisions as you, when it comes to their love life. Not everyone wants to move quite as fast as you can in a new relationship.

So if and when you sense that the person you're involved with romantically is not moving quite as fast as you, ask Archangel Ariel for help. Her clean and fresh energy will help you blow out any cobwebs of resentment.

Venus is also about money, and having Venus in Aries means you can make a lot of money fast. However, as you might have noticed, it means you can *spend* a lot of money fast, too. Once again, be glad you have Archangel Ariel on your side and ask her for help if and when your budget is blowing out. Remember, Archangel Ariel is an expert in manifestation, so call upon her if you need to manifest more cash. (And one more disclaimer: She's not a heavenly ATM machine. Far better to ask for help finding a well-paid *job* than for help winning the lottery!)

Mars in Aries

Now here is a combination to write home about! Mars is the planet of fire and war, and Aries is the *sign* of fire and war. Don't be alarmed! Just because you have Mars in Aries doesn't mean you will end up in a bloody battle! However, it can, and often does, mean you have a pretty hot temper. Learning to keep it under control is one of your main life lessons.

Remember, Aries energy is all about youth, and Archangel Ariel's energy is all about lightness of being. Sometimes, especially when we are young, we are so filled with vim and vigor and so intent upon chasing our goals that we rush at things like the pro-verbial Aries Ram in a china shop!

If this sounds like you, then one of the best things you can do is accept yourself. Ask Archangel Ariel to help you love yourself, temper and all. And once you have started to work on your self-acceptance, think about channeling your energies into something more constructive. Archangel Ariel will give you guidance in finding the right outlet, if you ask.

One very obvious way to release the intense Mars-in-Aries energies that course through you is via sport. Aries is all about going faster, and Mars has a fighter's style. Release your pent-up energy through rigorous exercise.

Because Mars-in-Aries people can be rather quick to anger, do ask Archangel Ariel for help with defusing tense conver-sations with humor.

It's amazing how an argument can be stopped in its tracks if someone cracks a joke or even just smiles. Anytime you feel yourself becoming upset, breathe in and ask Archangel Ariel to cool you down. It's better than counting to ten!

For the record, Mars-in-Aries lovers tend to be quick to connect and full of fiery passion!

Ascendant (Rising Sign) in Aries

People with a Rising sign in Aries are exciting, hot-blooded, and competitive. They exude the sprightly energies of Ariel *and* Aries. They're usually very nimble and light on their feet, fine-featured, and difficult to keep up with. Aries is guided by the planet Mars, which is the masculine principle. That means that if you have Aries Rising, you need to work just that much harder to keep your cool when you're challenged. (Don't worry . . . you can do it!)

There's a reason why you incarnated as an Aries Rising in this lifetime. It means that learning to control your temper is one of the lessons your soul decided to take on and hopefully master. Your Rising Sign's guardian angel, Ariel, has a much easier temperament, so if you do find yourself getting hot under the collar, speak to her. (Of course, the other thing you can do when your anger rises is embrace Ariel's outdoorsy energy—remove yourself from the place of upset and get outside in the fresh air so that you can bring your energies back into balance.)

This is a lovely Ascendant to have, because it means you can flit through life like a butterfly through an endless forest. Your Aries Rising can give you a need for speed, and sometimes you can even go too fast for those around you. That's when you can call upon Archangel Ariel to bring you back to a safe pace. Not that Ariel likes to go slowly, but she always has your best interests at heart, so if you need to curb your speed as you travel through life, she will help you. For example, if you feel you could benefit from learning to meditate, ask Ariel for assistance.

* * *

You can call upon Chamuel for any of the following, no matter what your sign is:

1. When you have lost your way

2. When you have lost a physical item

3. If you feel stuck in life, unable to move forward

4. When you need to find the money for a necessity

5. When you need to find the money to treat yourself to a luxury

6. If someone is being stubborn with you

7. If—truth be told—you know it's *you* who's being stubborn

8. When you're looking for true love

9. When you want to have confidence about your appearance

10. When you want to reconnect with a long-lost friend

11. When you want to reconnect with a friend after an argument

12. When you are seeking better-paid work

13. If you feel that your life is lacking in creature comforts

14. If you feel that you are becoming overly materialistic

15. If you feel stuck in a rut

16. When you are being lazy

17. If you want to live a more organic life

18. When you need help with goal-setting

19. When you have issues related to cash or property

20. If your self-esteem needs a boost

CHAPTER TWO

TAURUS AND ARCHANGEL CHAMUEL

* * * * * * * * * * * * * * * * * *

April 21–May 21

Taurus is the sign associated with the planet of love and luxury, as well as pleasure and art: Venus. If Taurus is very strong in your chart (that is, it's your Sun, Moon, or Rising sign), then Venus is also strong in your chart. So which archangel goes hand-in-hand with this Divine energy? Chamuel—a truly blessed archangel, who's also strongly associated with helping people find love and much more. That's the very soft and romantic side of Taurus. The flip side, of course, is the more intense Bull. As you might know, that's Taurus's symbol! Like raging bulls, Taureans are famous for being very stubborn when they want to be, especially in the pursuit of their desires. Taurus also has a temper, which you'll never see until it builds up and explodes like a volcano. Whichever part of your chart Taurus guides, that's where you can be rather stubborn and temperamental.

Happily, Archangel Chamuel is on hand to help. Like all archangels, Chamuel can help with anything you ask for assistance with, but his "special subjects" include helping you in your lifelong quest for satisfying relationships, friendships, and careers, along with inner peace. This is a perfect match with Taurus, guided by loving Venus, a planet obsessed with love and soul-mate relationships.

These two energies—Taurus and Archangel Chamuel—are in some ways very similar. For example, as the second astrological sign, Taurus is considered a very young sign. Think of a baby, crawling away to see the world—to discover new things—and wanting to "taste life," often literally. This matches

the energy of Chamuel, who is about *seeking*. Both relate to searching for the pleasures of life. But whereas Taurus will often look to outside creature comforts and to other people for fulfillment of their sensual desires, Archangel Chamuel reminds us that everything we seek is already *inside* us.

No matter what your sign, if you're having trouble in a relationship or a friendship, Chamuel is a great archangel to turn to for help. Sometimes your friends may be so caught up in their busy lives that they have no idea that you're feeling lonely and need them. Taurus is often reluctant to ask for help or for a hug, because Taureans are used to being the ones who are giving and who are exercising control. Archangel Chamuel can help you show vulnerability and let go of control issues, while revealing your true feelings to trustworthy friends.

Patient Taurus offers very steady, true love. Chamuel will help you find a way to reconnect with your friends, even after an argument. Dependable Taurus knows that real love is never fickle. Archangel Chamuel will help you find a way to make things work with *anyone*, if you're coming to the relationship from your heart and not your ego.

And you don't have to be Taurean to make the most of the Heavenly gifts that Archangel Chamuel has to offer. Chamuel can help with romantic relationships as much as with friendships. Taurus is not the sign that's associated *specifically* with love, and Chamuel is not the angel associated *specifically* with romance, but between the two of them, they create a wonderful combination for helping you on the path to true love. So if you're single and looking for love, remember to ask Archangel Chamuel to help you. He's known for helping people find their soul mates.

If you're attached, you can still work with Chamuel, asking him to help your relationship improve. That is, this archangel can help you if you're seeking love, and also if you're looking for a way to make it work with your current partner. Just ask for his assistance.

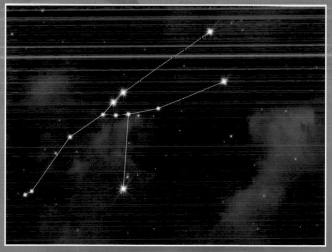

Archangel Chamuel can also assist with your career. This archangel is well known for helping people find the right line of work. If you're feeling lost professionally, he's the archangel to call upon, as one of his primary missions is to guide people to find careers that bring about personal and financial satisfaction. This dovetails very nicely with Taurus, the sign that loves its creature comforts more than most.

Archangel Chamuel can help you find the work you love, which will lead to creating abundance that you and your family can all enjoy. So if you feel stuck on your career path and unsure of what to do, turn to Chamuel. He actually wants to assist you in "working your Venus." And guess what? Venus is the

planet of riches! Ask Archangel Chamuel to help you find a way to generate the income you want so that you can enjoy the finer things in life.

Taurus is not a superficial sign in any way, but it's very much about beauty and beautiful things. For example, Taurus loves anything that is natural and real. That is, Taurus will always choose natural fibers over polyester, or a luxury resort over a motel. Fortunately, Archangel Chamuel can help you afford the beautiful things you need.

And if all this talk about money is making you uncomfortable, remember that we have incarnated here as humans to experience the spiritual *and* the material. Taurus combines the two, but is especially gifted at helping us have the best of the best in all areas. When we do what we love, the money follows.

Just be cautious about Taurus's tendencies to overindulge in food and spending. Archangel Chamuel can help you find true inner peace, which can never come from eating or shopping.

If the problem in your career is that you just haven't determined what you were "meant" to do, know that Archangel Chamuel is also very adept at helping you find your life purpose, no matter what your sign. Abundant Taurus/Venus can work well with Chamuel in this way. Just ask Chamuel for help whenever you're feeling lost and in need of Divine guidance.

Another of Archangel Chamuel's talents is helping you find things, including lost objects. So if you do the "Taurus thing" and accumulate some lovely items and then you lose one . . . well, now you know which angel to turn to! How very practical—and a lucky thing for Taureans, who have a constant need to know, "Where's my stuff?"

Chamuel is known for being very loving and sweet, despite coming under the sign of the Bull. And of course, there's nothing sweeter than Venus, who is all about love and kindness.

An interesting point to note about the Chamuel/Taurus synergy is that while Chamuel is the archangel who is about seeking, Venus represents the feminine principle, and as such, is about *attracting*. If you find that you're scared to go out and get what you want on any level, ask Archangel Chamuel for the courage to start your search. Also, remember that wherever you have Taurus ruling your chart is where you're prone to being stubborn. Archangel Chamuel knows that stubbornness stops the natural flow, so ask him for help when you sense that you're impeding your own progress.

Sun in Taurus

If your Sun is in Taurus, you're a born pleasure seeker. Not a thrill seeker, but a *pleasure seeker*. It's important to note the difference! You long for lovely, long afternoons with someone you love; a massage; time on your own for some self-indulgence; a walk in the park; or a relaxing period when you can sit down and read a book. You almost certainly do *not* like to be hurried, and will often dig your heels in the moment anyone tries to get you to move faster!

Don't worry—Archangel Chamuel isn't going to urge you to speed. But his energy *will* keep you moving, reminding you that you need to make an effort to find whatever you're seeking in this life.

On the other hand, one of the lessons that Archangel Chamuel will teach you is that while it's wonderful to seek pleasures and even "things" in the material world, what really counts is that you have a joyous heart. Chamuel will guide you to *what really matters:* true Divine love from God, which can be shared in a spiritually based relationship. Chamuel will also help you appreciate natural beauty in the sky, on the land, and in the sea.

The close association between Taurus and Venus, the planet of love, means that as you travel along your life's journey, everything you seek will eventually come to you . . . if you radiate the belief that you're worth it! Ask Archangel Chamuel for help in increasing your feelings of self-worth if you need more confidence and the ability to value yourself.

If Aries is the "newborn" of the chart, then Taurus is the baby who's learning to crawl and seek some independence. As people go out in the world as children, they look for the love they hopefully felt at home. Archangel Chamuel can help you find everything your heart is seeking—from love, to a happy home, to enough money to travel the world (if that's what you desire).

Yes, angels are spiritual beings, but one of their missions is to help us humans enjoy our lives and live happily and comfortably as we learn our soul lessons!

If you're struggling to pay your bills, it may be that you have soul lessons to learn about abundance. Perhaps that's one of the reasons why you incarnated as a luxury-loving Taurean in this lifetime. So don't be afraid to ask Archangel Chamuel for assistance with this. There's nothing "unholy" about living well, especially if you give to charities and other deserving causes. Learn to ask Archangel Chamuel for help with everything you're "seeking."

As the archangel who guides your chart, he's truly there for you.

Moon in Taurus

The Moon is what "feeds" you emotionally. When your Moon is in Taurus, you want the best of everything, and hopefully you're aware that you deserve it—we all do! Whatever you're striving for in life, rate yourself highly and the Law of Attraction will draw it to you with your self-belief. You might wonder how this works. Remember that the Law of Attraction states that "like attracts like." So if you radiate a strong belief that you deserve the best, then of course you're going to *attract* the best.

It's interesting to note that when it comes to Moon-in-Taurus individuals and what they consider the best, it's not necessarily about bling and flashy treasures. Taurus Moons are far more excited about being able to afford excellent, organic produce or comfortable furniture covered with fabulous natural fibers.

Archangel Chamuel is about seeking things out, so whether you're searching for an excellent restaurant where you can dine, or some other "creature comforts," you definitely have angelic support in your quest. Of course, you don't want to go overboard with your need for things—if you ever find yourself tipping into excess materialism, ask Chamuel to help you take a step back. Sometimes Taureans become overly concerned with acquiring material objects or worry about money. If you sense an imbalance, the Heavenly energies of Archangel Chamuel can help your focus be more spiritual and less material.

Having your Moon in Taurus is actually a great blessing. Astrologically, the Moon is very "happy" in this sign. As you may know, the Moon is about your emotions, and here, the Moon is "colored" by strong and even-keeled Taurus, so your emotions tend to be steady. This alone can make you very popular, as your friends delight in not having to second-guess your moods every day.

Next, we should mention one of the challenges for anyone with a Taurus Moon (or for whom Taurus is strong in their chart): you can be quite stubborn! While tenacity, sticking to your beliefs, and commitment to relationships and projects are highly admirable Taurean traits, stubbornness comes from the ego. If you recognize yourself in this description, ask Archangel Chamuel for help. His ability to heal and strengthen relationships of all kinds will work wonders and make you even more popular.

A little bit of self-awareness around this, coupled with prayers to Chamuel, can assist you in overcoming this hurdle. Don't be too hard on yourself when you know you've been hot-headed. We are all on Earth to learn lessons, and allowing things to go with the flow is one of yours.

People who incarnate with a Taurus Moon have a need to excel. They yearn for the finer things in life, and they're not afraid to put in the long, steady effort required to make that possible. Remember to ask Chamuel for help in whatever you're working on or aiming for. He's there to help you find what you desire, and to help you fulfill your emotional needs, including your aim to succeed.

Mercury in Taurus

Mercury is the planet of communications and the mind. Your Mercury guides how you think, speak, write, and otherwise express yourself. Having your Mercury in the slow and steady sign of Taurus means that pretty much no matter what else is going on in your chart, you have a mind that can't and won't be rushed, that takes its time to come to its own steadfast conclusions. So no matter what drama surrounds you, no matter what curveballs people are throwing at you, you should find it easy to stay centered and gather your thoughts.

The archangel guiding your Mercury is Chamuel, the angel who is all about seeking and finding. Of course, the two go very well together. Can't think of a word? Ask Archangel Chamuel, who is your heavenly dictionary and thesaurus and can help you find anything, including the right words at the right time.

One of the possible issues resulting from having Mercury in Taurus is that Taurus does have rather a stubborn energy. So you need to be careful not to allow yourself to get so entrenched in your thoughts and beliefs that you become inflexible. Don't get bogged down in facts, either. Allow your mind to soar at times! If you know you have a tendency to be a little intractable, ask Archangel Chamuel to help you out. Remember, the better we communicate, the better our lives are! Some Mercury-in-Taurus people find it easier to communicate through artistic mediums—for example, if you want to say "Thank you" or "Sorry" to someone, then draw them a card.

When it comes to using your planet Mercury for exams and presentations, you should find it easy to commit things to memory and keep them there. If in doubt, ask Archangel Chamuel to boost your brainpower. In addition, Archangel Chamuel will help you if you need Divine guidance. Just ask.

Venus in Taurus

Venus is the planet of love and abundance. And Taurus is the sign of steadfastness, pleasure, and sensual delights. It's a lovely combination to have in your birth chart. Of course, Venus, the goddess of love, can be a little flighty and fickle at times. But you have Venus in Taurus, one of the most down-to-earth signs of all. This means you can make the most of all Venus's gifts more easily than many. You are loyal in love. You take your time with love. And once you do love, you love long and truly, giving your partner pleasure in all kinds of ways. Venus loves to love, and Taurus brims with sensuality.

Venus also rules riches and luxury—having Venus in Taurus endows you with the ability and motivation to make the money needed to buy yourself all the creature comforts you could desire!

The archangel ruling your Venus is Archangel Chamuel. One of this angel's assigned roles is helping us mere mortals to fulfill our life goals. If you find yourself getting too caught up in the desire for earthly luxuries and comforts, talk to Archangel Chamuel, who will remind you that you have riches in your heart worth more than anything material.

On the other hand, if you haven't quite mastered the art of drawing luxury and comfort into your life, talk to Archangel Chamuel about helping you out. There is nothing wrong with generating enough money so that you can have what you want for yourself and your family! Archangel Chamuel is great at helping you find the right career path, so talk to him if you need to change jobs to earn more cash.

Similarly, if you are seeking love—be it from a partner or friend; your child, mother, father, or extended family; or anyone else—talk to Archangel Chamuel. He is there to help you with all love matters. Also, talk to him if you have issues with jealousy, something that does come up with possessive Taurus energy.

Mars in Taurus

"Slow and steady wins the race" could be your motto with your racy planet Mars in slow and steady Taurus. In one way, these two are rather opposite energies. Mars is the planet that gets out there and makes things happen—all about drive and determination, motivation, and getting the brass ring at all costs. Taurus, on the other hand, is the sign that likes to sit back in the sun and enjoy life, take it easy, and allow things to come rather than chasing them.

This astro-combo allows to you to take your time to get clear about your goals. You don't race off half-baked—or half-anything! Rather, Mars in Taurus knows that it's far better to keep your eye on the prize as you work slowly and steadily toward it.

The archangel guiding your Mars is Chamuel. Remember, much of Chamuel's energy is about seeking what you want in life. And that's the Mars energy, too. Chamuel does it with great love, and Mars in Taurus can do it with great style. When you're having trouble reaching a goal, talk to Archangel Chamuel and he will help you to get back on track.

Mars in Taurus can bring in an energy that sees you digging your heels in a bit, though, so be aware of that. When you know you're not allowing progress because you are somehow "stuck" in a personal or professional matter, ask Archangel Chamuel to help you keep things moving.

Mars is also the planet of sexual intimacy, as well as the planet of drive and determination, so having Mars in sensual Taurus means your lovers are in luck! You warm up slowly, but once you're switched on, you keep going. Since Chamuel is the archangel known for helping bring in soul mates, ask him for assistance if your intimate life is not really working for you. He is there to help!

Ascendant (Rising Sign) in Taurus

The Ascendant sign is the part of you that goes out into the world. It's the mask you wear when you're out in public, the face you show. It's not the real you—that's your Sun sign. Your Rising sign is the *you* that you reveal to the world. The presence of Taurus and Archangel Chamuel in this area is a wonderful thing.

The first reason why having Taurus Rising is a blessing is that it means Chamuel is one of the archangels who guides your chart. Archangel Chamuel's credo of "Go forth and seek what you need" allows you to be courageous. If you're Taurus Rising, you need never be afraid to go out into the world and seek whatever will make you happy. Of course, that means different things to different people. For some, it's about friends. For others, it's about having freedom. For still others, it's about amassing wealth and security. Chamuel will help you find what you're looking for—you just have to ask him.

On an astrological note, it's important to remember that having Venus so strong in your chart (Venus and Taurus go together) is also very useful to you. Remember, your Rising sign is the first thing people notice about you when they meet you. You have the planet of love, beauty, and kindness here. Yes, it means you come across as loving, beautiful, and kind—what a blessing!

And when it comes to work, the Taurus Rising/Archangel Chamuel combination is useful if you want to be a success in the business world. Just as Chamuel supports you in looking for what you want to magnetically draw to yourself this lifetime, Venus and Taurus combine to bring you good fortune, financial abundance, and other worldly gifts.

Do be aware—again—that Taurus Rising (like all Taurus energies) can bring stubbornness with it. When you find yourself totally stuck in a mood, negative thought pattern, or life rut, ask Archangel Chamuel to help you find your way out of it. Chamuel really is there to help you seek whatever you want in life—you just have to ask!

* * *

You can call upon Zadkiel for any of the following, no matter what your sign is:

1. When you need to forgive someone

2. When you need to remember someone's name

3. If you're about to complete an exam and need help with remembering the facts

4. When you have to write an important e-mail or letter

5. When you are going to initiate a very important conversation

6. To gain confidence

7. If you're trying to teach someone something

8. When you have an important research project to undertake

9. If you have to give a speech or presentation

10. To help you remember your true spiritual identity

11. When you need to shift your thoughts from negative to positive

12. To let go of pain from abusive relationships

13. If you're operating too much from your head and not enough from your heart

14. When you feel blocked emotionally

15. If you have to deal with a tricky, touchy subject

16. When you need to lighten up a bit

17. If someone has criticized you hurtfully and you're wondering how to respond

18. To heal a grudge

19. To remember where you put something

20. To improve your clairaudient abilities

CHAPTER THREE

GEMINI AND ARCHANGEL ZADKIEL

* * * * * * * * * * * * * * * * * * *

May 22–June 21

At first glance, Archangel Zadkiel and Gemini, the Air sign, might seem to make a strange pair. Zadkiel is the archangel of compassion and forgiveness, while Gemini is the astrological *flirt!* Archangel Zadkiel is about forgiveness that comes from the heart; while Gemini is associated with the intellect, the mind, and a talkative conversation style.

Despite their apparent differences, Archangel Zadkiel and Gemini actually work very well together because Archangel Zadkiel lends Gemini vital support and help.

Before we get into the more intense side of these two, let's look at some of their lighter "connections." For one thing, Archangel Zadkiel is known as the Archangel of Memory. Like Gemini, he's associated with learning and teaching. It's said that Archangel Zadkiel can help us remember both the practical and the esoteric.

If you have a lot of Gemini in your chart (your Sun, Moon, or Rising sign), there's a good chance that you'll spend your life researching, learning, and studying. Do remember that Archangel Zadkiel is available to help you succeed in your mental pursuits. Ask him for help with projects in your personal or private life.

If you have kids, teach them to connect with Archangel Zadkiel from an early age, no matter what their Sun sign. Being the "Archangel of Memory," he can help them recall facts and figures for exams, making school a lot easier!

The need to remember information involves more than studies, though. How about those times when you need to make a presentation at work, for

example (a very Gemini thing to do, since this sign is ruled by the communications planet, Mercury)? If you have Archangel Zadkiel on your side, helping you remember all the important points you need to make, you're obviously going to do a whole better than if you spend all your time looking down at your notes!

Wherever Gemini/Zadkiel is for you (Sun, Moon, or Rising) is where your thoughts flow more easily and where you can talk the leg off a table! The Gemini part of your chart is where ideas arise.

Moreover, those with Gemini strong in their charts have the ability to win friends and influence people because they're so engaging. These folks actually remember what they said to you the last time you met, and they remember *your* name and your kids' names, as well as where you said you spent your last vacation, for example. If you have the common habit of forgetting people's names, ask Archangel Zadkiel for assistance. Zadkiel and Gemini really work magic together when it comes to communicating. That's why so many Geminis are popular, and are also known as the most flirtatious of all the signs.

Another thing to bear in mind with Archangel Zadkiel is that he can help you shift your focus from the negative to the positive. If you find yourself in a downward thought spiral, ask Archangel Zadkiel for help. Of course, we all need to deal with our emotions, and no one's suggesting that you gloss over your worries. However, if you're spending too much time recalling painful memories, for example, or conjuring up the worst possible scenario for your future, ask Archangel Zadkiel to intervene, which will help you clear and refresh your memory bank. Focusing on the good things in life is the easiest way to positively involve the Law of Attraction.

In addition, Archangel Zadkiel is all about keeping an open mind, and Gemini relates to the urge to share ideas through reading, writing, and talking. But if it's difficult to be tolerant of someone who's very different from you, ask Archangel Zadkiel to help you open yourself up to new ideas. Remember: everyone is your teacher in their own way!

Interestingly enough, Archangel Zadkiel is strongly connected with forgiveness. Sometimes the Airy-ness of Gemini means that you end up living in your head rather than your heart. So call upon Archangel Zadkiel to help reconnect your heart and mind, if you know you're being too logical and not compassionate enough. This is especially important if others have hurt you and you know you need to forgive them.

Even if your heart is blocked, Archangel Zadkiel can help remind you that to err is human and to forgive is Divine. Even if it's not immediately obvious to you why you should forgive someone who's hurt you, on an intellectual level, it certainly does make sense to forgive. Geminis don't usually hold on to grudges, but Gemini-influenced people can sometimes move through life so fast that they just discard anyone who upsets them. Archangel Zadkiel will remind you that it's far better to work on restoring

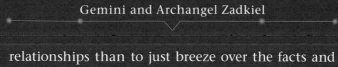

Gemini and Archangel Zadkiel

relationships than to just breeze over the facts and
find someone new to keep you company.

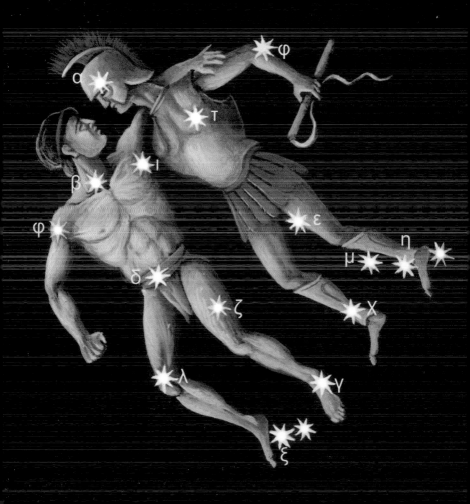

Sun in Gemini

Geminis have a very light touch in life, which is a wonderful quality. Some other signs tie themselves up in knots overthinking things, and lacking the confidence to take action. However, Geminis rarely have issues with moving forward. Not that they don't have deep feelings, but they can work through them more quickly than most, as they're very mentally agile.

In fact, this is why Geminis have an unjustified reputation for being superficial. So, Geminis, ignore your critics and detractors! They're probably just jealous of your amazing ability to think things through very quickly and easily and keep life moving along. Archangel Zadkiel works well with your energies because he helps you move on from past pain, and he keeps things light. Moving on from pain doesn't mean pretending things never happened. Rather, it's about processing issues and releasing them into the ethers via forgiveness, when it's warranted. Archangel Zadkiel will always help you in this way.

Admirably, Geminis are the least likely to harbor resentment of all the astrological signs. Of course, that matches Archangel Zadkiel's forgiving energies perfectly. If you do find yourself obsessing over an offense someone perpetrated against you, be sure to ask Archangel Zadkiel for help. He will hold your hand so you can release resentment and resume your happy-go-lightly ways!

If you're a Gemini, you're one of the most adaptable signs, partly because you don't get stuck in the past. But please don't expect perfection if you can't let go of *everything*. Very few can! Some people think we humans need to have a breakdown to have a breakthrough. You know otherwise. Archangel Zadkiel will support you in maintaining your light touch in life. He'll also help you be kinder to yourself.

Actually, it's a funny thing, but so many Geminis apologize for their Sun sign. Let it be said here: *you have nothing to apologize for!* Being a Gemini is a marvelous thing, so if there are parts of you that you're not happy with, work on them and ask Archangel Zadkiel for assistance in showing yourself compassion. Zadkiel will help you see your Divine inner light and spiritual attributes.

Moon in Gemini

If Gemini guides your Moon, then you need to communicate. Some people are happy to be in their own little bubble, but you like to get out in the world and talk to people: to friends and family, to colleagues, to people on talk radio, to strangers you meet as you go about your day, and to people on Twitter and Facebook you haven't met yet.

And if you're that rare, shy Gemini Moon, you get your fix through writing or being a classic bookworm. Even shy Gemini Moon individuals open up on the Internet to friends and strangers, where they can share something without intimidating face-to-face discussions. Both Gemini and Archangel Zadkiel are about mental processes. As long as you're being mentally stimulated, you're at least halfway to happiness.

Be aware that the Moon guides your emotions, and Gemini is a very changeable sign. For this reason, if you're feeling depressed, you can rest assured that you won't feel down for very long. If someone upsets you, you tend to forgive and forget quickly, partly thanks to the influence of Archangel Zadkiel, who's about forgiveness and compassion. So ask Archangel Zadkiel to intervene when you're feeling low and you'll resume your sunny outlook on life.

Sometimes Zadkiel gently guides Geminis to find a helpful person. This could be a friend or even a counselor. Once you've asked Archangel Zadkiel for help, keep your eyes and ears open to see where you're being directed. Other times you'll be guided to read something on the Internet or in a book, which will help you deal with your particular situation.

Having a Gemini Moon also means that your love life is fast moving. More than anything, you crave a partner to whom you're attracted intellectually *and* romantically! Good conversation and listening skills are essential to you in a partner. Archangel Zadkiel will help you with all of your relationships, and particularly encourage you to develop empathy for others as you zoom through life.

Mercury in Gemini

Talkative much? Most (not all, but *most*) Mercury-in-Gemini people can talk a blue streak! Mercury is the communications planet, and Gemini is the sign that loves to chat. Put them together and if you don't get a bit of a talking machine, then chances are you have someone who is a bit of a writing or thinking machine.

If you're reading this and thinking that you have Mercury in Gemini, but you are not at all a chatterbox, don't panic. Some Mercury-in-Gemini people have aspects in their charts that mean they *don't* talk constantly. These people, though, tend to excel in other ways when it comes to communications. For example, they might be great formal debaters, or they might be excellent at writing pitches and reports.

Whichever way this astro-combo gets expressed, it nearly always gives a person a very good brain. If you have this in your chart, you have an ability to communicate that's second to none. You can be highly articulate, even eloquent. Or you might just end up being a talker! If that's the case, that's fine, too. Certainly you are likely to have a very agile mind.

The angel who rules your Mercury in Gemini is Archangel Zadkiel. He is known as the Angel of Memory—with him by your side and your Mercury in Gemini, you can excel in anything and everything that requires you to do rote learning or memorizing. Exams and speeches can become your forte, so if you have ever doubted your potential in either of these two areas, it's time to realize the gifts in your birth chart.

You should find it relatively easy to stay mentally positive with Mercury in Gemini, but anytime your thoughts wander to the dark side, ask Archangel

Zadkiel for help. He will be there for you! Positive thoughts create a positive life.

Venus in Gemini

If you have Venus (which is all about love and abundance) in Gemini (which is all about communication), you almost certainly love to write, read, and/or talk; and you can probably make a lot of money through doing any of those things. Whenever you meet people, you come across as charming and entertaining.

You have the potential to be a great communicator. But you're also the person who posts too many status updates on Facebook. Luckily, you usually make them so funny that people forgive you (Gemini energy has a great sense of humor). You're the person who keeps talking on the phone when you should be doing something else. If you don't write a blog, you probably text a lot, and you love to read as well. You're probably very attached to your cell phone. (Sound at all familiar?)

Your Venus in Gemini is guided by Archangel Zadkiel, who helps you go through life without too much angst. One of Archangel Zadkiel's fortes is forgiveness. You're so lucky, because you tend not to hang on to hurts and slights. Instead, you're very much a "today is brand-new day" person (unless, of course, there are other things going on in your chart that make it harder for you to let go!). But on those rare occasions when you do find it more difficult to forgive and forget, ask Archangel Zadkiel for help.

Also, if you sometimes fear that you're being all style and no substance in your personal or professional life, ask Archangel Zadkiel to help you slow down. Ditto if you know you're being a bit cavalier with someone's feelings.

Venus in Gemini also bestows you with creative gifts. And it also makes you a big flirt. Overall, there are plenty of reasons to be cheerful that you chose this astro-combo when you incarnated this time around. Remember, Venus is about love *and* riches, so whenever you have any issues related to either, Archangel Zadkiel is your go-to angel.

Mars in Gemini

Mars is the planet that rules how you handle conflict—having Mars in Gemini suggests that if and when you find yourself at odds with someone, your preferred method of vanquishing them is to use your cutting wit. Ouch!

Gemini is the chatterbox sign of the heavens. Mars is the planet that gets things done. When you have Mars in Gemini, you think fast, you tear through your task lists (sometimes perhaps a little *too* fast), and you might have rather a quick temper!

The angel on your side to help you deal with your witty Mars in Gemini is Zadkiel, who brings forgiveness. This is very good news for you when you overstep the Mars mark. Mars in Gemini can be brash (though very exciting!). Suffice to say, you often go where others fear to tread. You ask the hard, searing, probing questions. You say the thing that everyone else is thinking but doesn't dare utter. In short, you sometimes "shoot from the lip"!

If you do find yourself in trouble because of what you said or wrote before thinking it through, ask Archangel Zadkiel to help you get out of trouble. Similarly, if you're about to go into a tricky meeting where you know it's going to be in your best interests to remain calm, ask Archangel Zadkiel to be there with you and for you, so that you count to ten before unleashing.

Don't worry—having Mars in Gemini is not *bad*. Being up front is a wonderful thing, and chances are, you are that to a T. However, if you know you have a tendency to go too far, talking to Archangel Zadkiel about learning to rein things in is one of the smartest things you can do for yourself (and others!).

As for the sexual aspect of Mars (Mars is the sexual-intimacy planet), your brain is often your most erogenous zone! You want a partner who stimulates your mind as much as anything else.

Ascendant (Rising Sign) in Gemini

Gemini Rising folks are great conversationalists and have the "gift of gab." There's never an awkward silence around those with this Rising sign! Once you're at ease with someone, you're the person most likely to keep a conversation moving along.

Some people may accuse you of being so Gemini-Rising-Go-Lightly that you're actually superficial. They say you're the sort of person who, when chatting with someone at a party, is looking over your shoulder for someone more interesting to talk to. Does that sound at all familiar? If the very thought of this rankles, there might be a grain of truth to it, so see if you can work on this side of yourself. Many people don't like their Rising sign when they first find out about it, as it's the part of us that others see first, and we might prefer that they see something else!

So where does Archangel Zadkiel fit into this? Actually, he's your saving grace. While you may exhibit a somewhat shallow exterior (your Rising Sign is more or less your public mask), Zadkiel is the archangel who brings substance to your Rising sign. After all, Zadkiel is about forgiving and compassion, and Gemini is about communicating. So despite the Gemini reputation for spouting a lot of hot air, you're really that person who can talk your way through uncomfortable pauses and help everyone move to some kind of agreement. This is a huge gift, and something you would do well to be aware of, especially if you've had misgivings about your Rising sign.

Archangel Zadkiel can also help with your clairaudience if you're open to it. Clairaudience is when you receive auditory (sound) messages through spirit. Either you hear them in your head or others say things to you that really strike a chord. Developing your intuition is always a productive thing to do, and will stand you in good stead both personally and professionally. Many Geminis are naturally intuitive and have keen psychic abilities.

* * *

You can call upon Gabriel for any of the following, no matter what your sign is:

1. To heal issues with your parents

2. To receive guidance about child rearing

3. If you crave a family of your own

4. If you are having problems conceiving

5. When you want something for your family, like a bigger house or a vacation

6. When you have a big, important announcement to make

7. If you want to get your book published

8. When you have an important document to write

9. If you want a happier home life

10. When you are furnishing or redecorating a room for your children

11. When you need to overcome procrastination with respect to your priorities

12. When you're having problems buying or selling your home

13. When you need more time to nurture yourself

14. If you're spending all your time caring for someone else

15. When you need to reawaken your inner child and have some more fun

16. If you are artistic and want to progress creatively

17. If you dream of making your living through artistic pursuits

18. When you need help with an adoption process

19. To gain more confidence with big life changes

20. To develop closer relationships with Jesus and Mother Mary

CHAPTER FOUR

CANCER AND ARCHANGEL GABRIEL

* * * * * * * * * * * * * * * *

June 22–July 23

Those born under the constellation of Cancer are known as home lovers. Where Cancer falls in your chart is where you are also loyal, protective, sensitive, and sometimes moody.

Cancerians have a reputation for being wonderful stay-at-home cake-bakers who think only of their children, partners, and extended family members. And that is partially true! Cancer is the most family-oriented sign. However, if you know any Cancerians, you also know that they are very dynamic people! They're just as likely to be movers and shakers in the business world as they are happy to be stay-at-home parents. Cancerians are a wonderful mix of nurture and power, which is why they have the nurturing and powerful Gabriel as their ruling archangel. Before we go further, a small point: there's some debate over whether Archangel Gabriel is male or female. Certainly, the name works for either gender; and over time, Archangel Gabriel has been seen mostly as a male by churchgoers. However, in many of the beautiful early paintings of Gabriel, this archangel has long hair, has a female face and figure, and is wearing a dress. In this book, we're working on the premise that Gabriel is female.

Archangel Gabriel is probably best known through the biblical story of her appearance to Mary, when she announced that the Virgin would soon be with child. This story is known by just about everyone who went to Sunday school. It's one of the most famous biblical accounts, known as the "Annunciation." Archangel Gabriel said, "Mary, you have found favor with God. You will conceive and give birth to a son, and you are to call him Jesus."

This isn't the only time that Archangel Gabriel appears in connection with the birth of Jesus. She is also seen later on in the Bible bringing "good tidings of great joy" to the shepherds who adore Jesus in the manger shortly after his birth. Gabriel also brought miraculous news of a forthcoming birth to the elderly Zachariah and his wife, Elizabeth, who fulfilled this prophecy by giving birth to their son, John the Baptist.

Gabriel is the most family oriented of the archangels, and for this reason, fits very well with Cancer, the most family oriented of the astrological signs. After all, the sign of Cancer is Moon guided, and the Moon is also about motherhood and the home.

Not surprisingly, then, Archangel Gabriel (and the sign of Cancer) is strongly associated with pregnancy and child rearing. Gabriel leads hopeful parents toward child conception. And once someone has a child and is learning about parenthood and the wonders and challenges that go along with it, Archangel Gabriel helps all who ask.

The Archangel Gabriel/Cancer pairing is a very warm and comforting combination. If you have any Cancerian friends, you'll recognize how nurturing they are. Archangel Gabriel tends to be most strongly associated with children up to school age, after which Virgoan Metatron and Aquarian Uriel take over. So if you have very young children, ask Archangel Gabriel to look after them until they go to school, after which point you can ask Metatron and Uriel to care for them as they mature.

Also, Archangel Gabriel helps as much with adopted kids as she does with "birth children." If you want to adopt or you've already done so, be sure to ask Archangel Gabriel for help. She'll be there for you and your adopted child, especially through the difficult adoption process and the family issues that follow. Gabriel helps parents attain their highest potential with respect to their offspring.

Both Archangel Gabriel and Cancer focus on tenderness. Think of a mother suckling her young and you'll get a sense of the softness to which we're referring. But sometimes in relationships, Cancer can be needy and clingy.

Archangel Gabriel is also there for you when you want to get in touch with your inner child, which is something beneficial for all signs. If you've been working or worrying too much, this archangel can help you let go, play, and have fun. After all, the Creator didn't put you on Earth to struggle endlessly. Gabriel can help you balance your responsibilities with self-care and enjoyment.

And like a good mother, Archangel Gabriel also nudges you along your path as you mature. This trait matches the Cancerian energy. Cancer is a Cardinal sign, which means that nurturing involves nudging, teaching, and motivating your offspring! Good parents don't just let their children run amok. A good mother or father understands that children need guidance. Archangel Gabriel can also guide and motivate you, at any age.

Financial insecurity is another characteristic of those with the sign of Cancer strong in their charts.

Although they have healthy bank accounts, they worry about having enough money to meet their basic needs. And when Cancerians feel financially insecure, they become moody and grumpy.

Cancerians and strong Cancerian types (those with the Sun, Moon, or their Ascendant in Cancer) tend to be good earners *and* good savers. It's just a part of their makeup, because they want to be able to provide for their loved ones. In fact, for Cancerian types, there's never enough money for them to relax. They want more in the bank—not because they're showing off, but for financial security.

Archangel Gabriel can help here, too. She functions as a manager or agent for those who are "messengers," such as artists and writers. Whichever creative talent you possess, Archangel Gabriel can assist you in your career. Call upon Gabriel for help and guidance if you're in the arts, working in communications, or involved in anything to do with the delivery of spiritual messages.

Sun in Cancer

Each astrological sign is guided by a specific planet, and Cancer's "planet" is the Moon. Being

Cancerian means being Moon guided. This is a great thing, because it means you're far from stuck emotionally. That's the positive spin. The less positive take on being Moon guided is that you can be moody. You can be feeling "up" in the morning and "down" in the afternoon, before being "up" again in the evening. This is because you absorb the lunar energy more than most.

So, for example, the Moon harmonizes with Venus (up), then smacks up against Pluto (not so up), before harmonizing with Neptune (up). Does this mean you're a slave to your emotions? Hopefully not! And now that you know that beautiful Archangel Gabriel guides your Sun, maybe you'll learn to work with her calming energy. Just ask her for help in balancing your emotions. You may be guided to do morning meditations, enroll in a yoga class, or change your diet. (Everything we eat affects our moods.)

Archangel Gabriel is one of the most nurturing of the archangels. So if you do find that you're feeling less emotionally calm than you'd like, sit quietly and meditate with her. Ask her to bring you inner peace. Remember, Archangel Gabriel's name means "God is my strength," so when you need more power, you can ask her to help you. Cancerians are known as sensitive, sometimes anxious folks, so lean on Archangel Gabriel when it all gets to be too much. Part of your insecurity may come from being so attached to your family. You may care so much that it hurts at times. So when you have concerns about your loved ones, ask for help.

Archangel Gabriel is there for anyone in the arts. Call upon her for help, guidance, and "agenting" if you're currently (or desire to be) an actor, artist, author, dancer, journalist, model, musician, reporter, singer, songwriter, or teacher.

Moon in Cancer

Having a Cancerian Moon is a huge blessing. It makes you a soft and gentle person who is totally suited for parenthood. If you're unable to have children for any reason, spending time with your family and friends' children or fostering or adopting will work wonders for you. You may even transfer your parenting skills to working with animals or anyone who needs protection. You receive satisfaction from nurturing others.

Your Moon sign also reveals what you *need*. Having your Moon in Cancer means that you need to nurture and *be* nurtured. It's very easy and natural for you to focus on nurturing others. If you ask, Archangel Gabriel will help you find the answers to all your questions about how to best look out for others. And if you know that you're being overly nurturing in a dysfunctional and codependent way (something that many a Cancerian-type person falls victim to), Archangel Gabriel can help you there, too. Part of parenting is allowing your kids (and other people whom you nurture) to grow up and become self-sufficient.

Apart from that, Archangel Gabriel can help you with your children in more general ways. She's there for all moms and dads, and if you have a Cancerian Moon, you have an extra-special connection. Think of it as having Archangel Gabriel on speed dial.

In addition to nurturing others, you need to nurture *yourself.* Having a Cancerian Moon makes you extra sensitive to life's painful moments. So ask Gabriel to focus your attention on self-care and ensuring that the help you give to others is emotionally healthy and not codependent.

With Archangel Gabriel associated with your Moon, you also have a guardian angel related to working in the arts. If this is something you want to do or are doing, remember to talk to Archangel Gabriel when you're feeling unsure about your progress or your next step. Gabriel has opened amazing doors of opportunities for other human messengers, and she can do the same for you.

Mercury in Cancer

Mercury is the planet that focuses upon the way you talk, think, and write. Cancer is the caring and nurturing sign. Put them together and you have someone who sounds very caring when they talk. This is a massive godsend! As you might know, when it comes to communication, it's nearly all about *how* you say it, rather than what you actually say. If you

talk nicely to people, you're far more likely to get their attention.

That's the upside. However, having Mercury in Cancer also means you're prone to moodiness. Mercury is the planet of the mind; Cancer is ruled by the Moon that waxes and wanes. So the way your mind is working can wax and wane with the lunar cycle. One day you're up and optimistic, and the next you're worried that everything's going to collapse! Plus, sometimes you're a seemingly bottomless barrel of insecurities.

The angel guiding your Mercury in Cancer is Gabriel, which makes for a wonderful combination. Mercury is the planet of communications, and Gabriel is the archangel who gave one of *the* most famous communications of all: the Annunciation, when Blessed Mary learned she would soon become mother to Jesus.

Ask Archangel Gabriel to help you stay on an even mental keel. Keeping an eye on the Moon cycles can also help. As the Moon grows full each month, you might need to breathe deeper!

Not surprisingly, Mercury in Cancer is a great placement for anyone who wants to write or has to do so (for example, a professional writer or those who write reports as a part of their job or education). And it almost goes without saying that having Mercury in Cancer is wonderful for being a parent. Archangel Gabriel is strongly connected with family, as is the sign of Cancer. Having Mercury in Cancer also means you tend to be very intuitive, so ask Archangel Gabriel for help developing your intuition more fully in everyday life.

Venus in Cancer

Now here is a romantic astro-combo. Venus is the planet of love, and Cancer is one of the most sentimental signs in the heavens. Crabs do, of course, have a hard outer shell, but their soft underbelly makes them vulnerable!

So if you have Venus (the love and luxuries planet) in Cancer (soppy, sentimental, but still rather dynamic), you have a delightful, dreamy combination that will bring along with it a profound need for a happy home life.

People with Venus in Cancer make marvelous and devoted parents. Kids with Venus in Cancer tend to be gentle, soft-spoken, but moody!

If there's one potential trouble spot for people with this astro-combo, it's that you can sometimes be *ultra*sensitive and *overly* protective. So ask the angel who guides your Venus—Archangel Gabriel—for help with not taking things too personally! Archangel Gabriel can also be of assistance when you know you're being too clingy (a common Cancerian issue).

When it comes to your love life, if you have Venus in Cancer, (1) you're a bit of a pushover once you have given your heart away, and (2) you're a very loving and loyal partner. If you're single and looking for love, or if you and your partner are going through tough times, talk to Archangel Gabriel, who can help you work through any issues.

But if all that sounds like Venus in Cancer makes you a bit feeble, think again! Venus-in-Cancer people can also be very dynamic. Your Venus is also about how you relate to the idea of abundance. Cancer is one of the signs best equipped to make a very good living. Put them together and you get folks who can bring in a tidy sum, most of which they will probably want to spend on their loved ones—preferably on happy vacations together by the water, such as the sea, a lake, a river, or a pool. Talk to Archangel Gabriel anytime you have money worries.

Mars in Cancer

Mars is the planet of drive, determination, anger, and aggression. Cancer is the watery sign associated with the Crab, which scuttles off sideways at the first sign of trouble. So if you have Mars in Cancer, you may need to work on your ability to assert yourself.

On the upside, having Mars in Cancer means you know that sometimes the best way to go after your dreams is to go "sideways." You avoid confrontation. On the downside, having Mars in Cancer can mean you're sometimes so easily upset that you give up on things and people long before you should.

So when are you Big, Powerful Mars in Cancer instead of Timid Mars in Cancer? When the Moon is in the right place for you and the issue at stake is worth fighting over, you can dish it out just as much as you take it. In fact, at times, you can be downright argumentative. Moreover, if someone you love is placed in harm's way, you will react first and ask questions later every time.

The angel who guides your Mars in Cancer is Gabriel. So if you know you have a short fuse or you tend to argue just for the sake of it, you can ask Archangel Gabriel for help with dealing with these potential issues.

Similarly, if you tend toward being a conflict-phobic Mars-in-Cancer type who avoids confrontations, ask Archangel Gabriel for help with facing the battles you need to. No one would suggest go in all guns blazing all the time. However, some conflicts must be dealt with. Archangel Gabriel can help you go from meek to mildly willing to talk through any problems.

Note that Mars is also about sexual intimacy. Mars in Cancer usually makes for a person who needs to be quite in love for the sex to work well for them. We're talking sentimentality plus sensuality. Talk to Archangel Gabriel if you ever encounter intimacy issues.

Ascendant (Rising Sign) in Cancer

The Moon guides Cancer, and the Ascendant is about your appearance, so it's not surprising that many Cancer Rising people have round, Moonlike faces! The women also tend to be rather busty, as Cancer is the maternal sign associated with child-raising. Archangel Gabriel has a strong feminine energy, which fits in with the Cancer Ascendant nicely.

The nurturing side of Cancer is a strong trait in those who have this Ascendant. The Cancerian

Rising person welcomes you with a big warm hug, feeds you homemade soup and bread, and then beams lovingly at you as you talk after your meal. The Cancer and Archangel Gabriel combination results in a very warm exterior (remember, the Ascendant is your public persona).

If you're a dancer, model, singer, or any other artistic type who is in the public arena, this Rising sign is a real blessing. Even though Cancerians are known for being shy, the energy of Archangel Gabriel can really help you. Gabriel especially helps messengers and artists. So ask her for assistance anytime you have to go onstage or perform in public. Ditto, of course, if you're a writer of some kind and you have writer's block.

Cancer Rising people are very expressive with their emotions, and since Archangel Gabriel concentrates upon communication, you have a Heavenly blessing in this regard.

* * *

You can call upon Raziel for any of the following, no matter what your sign is:

1. When you want to heal a karmic relationship
2. When you want to understand the esoteric more deeply
3. When you want to remember your past lives
4. When you want to get someone's attention
5. To interpret your dreams
6. To help you remember your dreams
7. When you want to communicate with someone in heaven
8. To improve your psychic abilities
9. To open your mind and heart to other dimensions
10. To help you teach or write about spirituality
11. If you know that your ego is getting out of control
12. To get information about ancient secrets and wisdom
13. To get closer to God
14. To learn how to "automatic-write" messages from the Divine
15. To balance your karma
16. To understand and heal phobias
17. To uncover the basis of chronic conditions and patterns
18. To do past-life regressions on others
19. To let go of negative patterns and toxic relationships
20. To manifest your dream career as a spiritual teacher

CHAPTER FIVE

LEO AND ARCHANGEL RAZIEL

★ ★ ★ ★ ★ ★ ★ ★ ★ ★ ★ ★ ★ ★ ★ ★

July 24–August 23

Archangel Raziel has a rainbow-colored aura that beautifully complements the sign of Leo, guided by the Sun. Without the Sun, there's no rainbow . . . and without the rainbow? Well, life would be less enchanting! So, too, would the world be less colorful without the wonderful personality-plus Leos!

And Archangel Raziel adds even more beauty to the Leo picture. Like the Sun, Raziel shines. Like the rainbow, Archangel Raziel is radiant. Wherever you have Leo in your chart is where *you* can light it up.

Leo is all about drama and showmanship. This is the sign that guides actors—and the attendant drama—on television, onstage, and in the movies. The drama can sometimes extend to real life, as Leos can be "drama queens" or divas, or demand to be the center of attention. Think of a grand entrance where everyone cranes their neck to see someone, and you have an image and feeling of Leos in all their glory.

Think of the Leo symbol: the Lion, king of the jungle . . . the epitome of Leo fabulousness. Leos have never been the shrinking violets of astrology. By the same token, Raziel is one of the most showy archangels. The glories of Heaven are visible in the beautiful prism-of-light rainbow that surrounds Raziel and which reflects the Leo Sun.

As the wizard and metaphysician of the archangels, Raziel has the power to heal. And so, too, do Leos or those with a strong Leo bias in their charts, whether they know it or not. They have the ability to entertain and literally en-*light*-en people. Think of the actor on the stage who helps audience members forget all their troubles as he struts his stuff. Archangel

Raziel can also help people heal their painful pasts if they ask. By the same token, time spent with a Leo can distract us from ourselves. For one thing, Leos are very happy to talk about themselves!

Leos are often teased for thinking that they are at the center of the Universe. But considering that their sign's planet is the Sun, it's only natural that they feel that things "revolve" around them, the way that the planets revolve around the Sun. But the upside of Leos is their extreme warmth and generosity of spirit. They might have a "Look at me!" theme (showbiz queen Madonna is an example), but their own confidence can inspire us to feel more confident about ourselves.

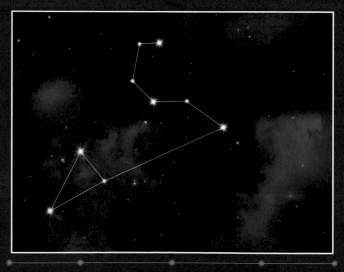

Leos live by the maxim "There's nothing enlightened about shrinking so that other people won't feel insecure around you." People with strong Leo energy in their charts are grand in many ways, including in their magnanimousness and generosity. They're hardly ever petty. Instead, they help us raise the bar on our own personal standards. If we spend time with Leos and end up feeling worse about ourselves, that's really our problem, not theirs! Archangel Raziel is about healing our neuroses, after all.

Leo is also the sign that doesn't ever dwell upon the past. The Sun never goes retrograde (unlike Mercury, Venus, and Mars). This so beautifully complements the energy of Archangel Raziel, who helps us deal with the past—not by wallowing in it, but by forging a path to the future. In fact, Archangel Raziel helps us heal in all directions of time, including our past lives and childhood emotional wounds. Think of the Leo Sun shining and bringing illumination where there was once darkness and fear. This is how Archangel Raziel can heal us wherever we have Leo in our charts.

Similarly, Leos do tend to wear their hearts on their sleeves. But by being so showy and visible, they open themselves up to criticism. This is a part of their charm and their famed big-heartedness.

By the same token, Archangel Raziel helps us heal deep-seated hurts by peeling away layers of pain we've accumulated.

So, if you have emotional pain that needs healing, Raziel is the archangel you should call upon for forgiveness and releasing the past.

Because they tend to be so open, Leos are famous for being blunt and to the point. A little-known secret about Leos, though, is that the Lion also has a tiny kitty-cat inside. Leos tend to take things *very* personally, and other people's remarks can really cut deep, even if Leos don't show it. Misunderstanding and miscommunication cause relationship issues for Leos, so if you have a lot of this sign in your chart, ask Archangel Raziel for help if and when you feel slighted or your pride is hurt. And be sure to double-check what people really mean when you hear them say something that appears to be hurtful. It could be that you've misunderstood the other person, who was trying to say something nice in an awkward way.

Raziel also informs people about esoteric subjects. He's the archangel who can help us understand spiritual symbolism, past lives, dream interpretation, sacred geometry, and other profound topics. Compare this with the astrological symbol of the

Sun, which is aligned with Leo. The Sun shines a bright light wherever it goes. Think of the tarot card "The Sun," and you'll get a sense of how Archangel Raziel and Leo work together, bringing light and understanding where there has been confusion.

Leos set people straight—they're not sugarcoaters. Rather, they're usually straight-shooters and easy to understand. They might have a reputation for being overly bold at times, but at least you know where you stand with them. They don't hide their light under a bushel, and neither does Archangel Raziel!

Some people do find the attention-seeking aspect of Leos a little hard to deal with. But like our Creator, we are meant to shine! This is very much a part of the Leo/Archangel Raziel credo.

Archangel Raziel encourages you to step out of the shadows and exercise your inner Leo. If you're passionate about a world issue, for instance, Archangel Raziel can help you summon the courage to speak publicly about the topic. Raziel will help you feel comfortable about being in the spotlight, especially if you're teaching about spirituality or healing. Just ask for his assistance and he's there.

If you're unsure about how to work with Archangel Raziel, ask him to help you in your dreams.

Like the bright Sun of Leo that lights the way for the astrological wheel, Archangel Raziel will work with you while you sleep to help you "see the light" of the spiritual truths your soul is seeking to understand.

Sun in Leo

Leos are famed for being very bright and bold "up-front" people. If you've incarnated as a Leo, there's probably not a lot that intimidates you. It's really a blessing to have your Sun in Leo, but it's also a form of responsibility. In many ways, you're one of the people on this planet who's meant to lead others. The Sun was once considered to be the center of the Universe, but although we've since discovered otherwise, you are still the celestial body at the center of our solar system. Therefore, you are one of the signs that others look to for guidance.

You're the person who turns heads and stands out, and you were born to be a star. That matches perfectly with beautiful Archangel Raziel, whose rainbow-colored aura is reminiscent of a peacock oh-so-proudly strutting his array of feathers. If you're one of those Leos who doesn't like the spotlight, though, then Raziel can help you overcome this (if that's your desire), or let your *work* be in the spotlight (such as products that you've created). Archangel Raziel can help you heal your insecurities so you can become the person you know you're meant to be!

Archangel Raziel can also impart mysterious, esoteric information to you. If you're interested in learning more about the spiritual secrets that have been passed down through time, talk to Raziel and ask for his help. He is there for you!

Working with clear quartz crystals that mimic Raziel's beautiful rainbow aura can also be helpful. If you feel guided to do so, display or hang clear quartz crystals where you'll frequently see them so that you're reminded of your ability to work with the unseen. You'll also be rewarded with dazzling rainbows on sunny days.

And if you're a Leo in your full power who's unafraid to be seen, thank Archangel Raziel and enjoy your lifetime dance in the center of the Universe!

Moon in Leo

Those born with their Moon in Leo have a tangible need to be adored and admired. If you're talking to such people and you relay this factoid to them, they usually smile wryly and agree!

The good news for Leo Moon people is that your audience is enchanted with you. If you've read the previous sections about Leo and Archangel Raziel, you already know that Raziel has a wonderful rainbow-colored aura that makes him stand out anywhere. Just as you can't miss those with a strong Leo presence in their charts when they walk into a room, so too would Archangel Raziel stand out in any lineup of archangels! If you desire to shine more brightly (and Leo Moon people will almost always want *that*), ask Archangel Raziel to help you out.

On the other hand, balance is necessary so that your relationships run smoothly. If your need for recognition is giving you problems (such as causing you to be overly attention seeking or overpowering in relationships), ask Archangel Raziel to help you. He will be particularly adept at assisting you while you sleep, and can take you to classrooms in other dimensions while you dream. When you wake up, you might not fully understand Archangel Raziel's teachings or even consciously remember them, but you can be sure he's helped you, as you requested.

Some of the more advanced Leo Moon people understand that a part of what they are here on Earth to do in this lifetime involves helping others see life more clearly. If you feel that this is one of *your* roles, ask Archangel Raziel to guide you in helping and healing others. He can offer you deep spiritual understanding that you, in turn, can pass on to others.

And finally, if you find that you're wrestling with your "dark side" (we all have one, no matter what our Sun or Moon signs), once again ask healing Archangel Raziel to help you shine light into the darkest recesses of your personality. He can also help you be less defensive if you tend to take everything too personally, or if you find criticism where none was intended.

Mercury in Leo

If there's one Mercury placement that knows how to talk a good talk, it's Mercury in Leo! Mercury guides how we think and communicate. Leo is the sign of the center-stage superstar. Put them together and you have someone who comes across as anything from a charismatic raconteur and entertainer . . . to a downright know-it-all and even a bossy boots.

The angel who guides Mercury in Leo is Raziel, the archangel with the amazing rainbow-colored aura. Just like Raziel, Mercury-in-Leo people are attention getters—and sometimes attention seekers! If you know you have a tendency to want to hog the limelight, and you want to do something about that, talk to Archangel Raziel. Angels knows it's okay to shine, and Raziel would like you to know that, too. However, if you feel you need to tone things down, Archangel Raziel is there for you. This information can also be useful for parents with Mercury-in-Leo kids. If your child is a bit of a natural show-off and it's causing problems, ask Archangel Raziel for help.

Since it's so closely connected with the stage and screen, Mercury in Leo also gives you a natural ability to get up and talk, sing, present, act, and so forth in front of people. Plus, it's creative. If you have yet to embrace this side of yourself and wish you had

enough confidence to do so, ask Archangel Raziel for help. And even if you don't want to perform in public, Mercury in Leo can help you talk confidently in your private life in such a way that others will want to listen to you.

Archangel Raziel is also an angel with great healing powers, and having him as the angel guiding your Mercury means your words have great power to heal. In addition, he understands and teaches esoteric wisdom. Having your Mercury guided by him means you have great access to the wisdom of the ages. Seek it, and ask for his help when you need it on your path.

Venus in Leo

Venus is the planet that's about love, abundance, style, and grace. Having your Venus in Leo is a blessing. It means you're a person with an innate fashion sense. In fact, you probably make a fashion statement every morning when you dress yourself! Or your Venus in Leo comes out in your creative expression.

Moreover, you love looking good. And when it comes to love, you want your partner in life to look good, too. Venus-in-Leo people tend to be very drawn toward lovers others will *admire*. This is fine up to a point, of course, but could become a problem if you are looking too much for style over substance when it comes to your relationships. It's what's on the inside that counts with partners!

The angel guiding your Venus is Archangel Raziel. He exudes all of the colors of the rainbow, so he understands the power of aesthetics. However, if you know you have issues with vanity, if you're spending more than you can afford on your wardrobe, or if you would like to find a way to boost your income so you can *afford* to spend more, talk to Archangel Raziel. He will not judge you for wanting to look your best.

Your Venus in Leo also guides you in money matters. Leo is a very generous sign. In theory, the more money you make, the better, since you know that as the center of your own universe, you deserve nothing but the best.

If you fall on hard financial times and you need help, ask Archangel Raziel for assistance. Also talk to Archangel Raziel if you like to take chances with your cash—perhaps it's about buying too many lottery tickets, or making risky investments in get-rich-quick schemes. Actually, you have natural good luck when it comes to cash, but don't blow it or push it too far! Use your intuition as only a Venus-in-Leo person can, to find smart, glamorous investments.

Mars in Leo

Confident much? Mars is the planet of drive and determination. When you want something and you decide to go out and get it, it's your Mars that is the engine driving you. And you have this powerful, fiery planet in the powerful, fiery sign of Leo. This combination gives you confidence galore. Mars-in-Leo people can be larger-than-life and have a temper to match!

Leo is not naturally a very angry sign; rather, Leo has a sort of noble quality to it. Losing your cool is not very gracious, and people with a lot of Leo energy in their chart know it. But Mars is brash and only interested in what it wants.

If you have Mars in Leo, there could be times when you forget all about the idea of being gracious and become verging on selfish. You *could* say this is a wonderful thing, and it's not that you're being ruthless—you're just very clear about what you want!

But if you're elbowing people out of your way as you go about your life mission, you'll feel in your soul that this isn't the highest-vibrational path of manifestation. The angel to talk to is Raziel. Ask Archangel Raziel to shine his bright and beautiful light into your life so that you can find success in a gracious way.

With driven Mars in show business–y Leo, you have celestial support if you want to entertain, perform, or otherwise become a well-known star in your field, no matter what it is. Mars in Leo is also very creative in every way. Talk to Archangel Raziel and ask for guidance on your path.

Finally, Mars is also the sexual-intimacy planet. Having Mars in Leo means—similar to having Venus here—that you want partners who look good and make you feel special because you have them by your side. You seek someone who can bring out your inner child, too. If your intimate life is in a slump, talk to Archangel Raziel. He's there to help . . . with everything.

Ascendant (Rising Sign) in Leo

Having Leo Rising is a huge blessing, as long as you're comfortable being a highly visible and memorable human being! The Leo Rising individual has an energy that demands attention. Similarly, Archangel Raziel is also intensely vivid, thanks to his rainbow-colored aura. It's very hard for you to go unnoticed, that's for sure. So the question is: what are you going to do with all this attention?

Being noticed for its own sake isn't going to do you any good. You need to have a clear mission that will benefit from all the attention bestowed upon you. That's where Archangel Raziel can help you. He's a wizard who's privy to secret information and mysteries. Ask Raziel to help you choose a cause that stirs your passion (helping children, women, animals, the environment, and so on) and to teach you all you need to know about this topic. In this way, you can become a font of wisdom for those who are eager to listen to you.

The best thing about having Leo as your Rising Sign is that it endows you with marvelous dignity, courage, and integrity. You're viewed by others as generous and highly attractive. But this wonderful exterior can mask deeper insecurities that need healing. Remember that Leo is the sign of acting, and the Rising sign is the mask you wear. Archangel Raziel is highly skilled in helping heal any and all neuroses, such as a confident façade. Ask Archangel Raziel to help you deal with your self-esteem issues, as well as any past lives that might be adversely affecting you today.

You come across as warmhearted, and your generosity of spirit can actually be healing to others who spend time with you. So ask Archangel Raziel to embed ideas into your psyche that you can share with others in a positive way.

* * *

You can call upon Metatron for any of the following, no matter what your sign is:

1. When you feel that your aura and chakras need clearing

2. If you need a miracle in order to get somewhere on time

3. When you want to learn more about the spiritual side of life

4. To get more motivation to exercise

5. If you're feeling like you're not "in your body" enough and need grounding

6. If you're thinking too hard and not feeling enough

7. To get the motivation to detox, and to *stay* detoxed

8. When you want to analyze a situation

9. For those days when you are too self-critical

10. For help clearing out stagnant energy from your home

11. If you're feeling guided to eat more healthfully but not doing it

12. When you're doubting your own self-worth

13. When you're called upon to teach someone something

14. If you have too much on your plate to handle

15. To engage in remote viewing (that is, finding out information via extrasensory perception)

16. If you're trying to find a natural remedy to a health issue or an alternative-health practitioner

17. To let go of blocks to manifestation

18. If you fear you're going to miss an important deadline

19. When you're doing something that requires great attention to detail

20. When you want to get some healthy routines in your life

CHAPTER SIX

VIRGO AND ARCHANGEL METATRON

* * * * * * * * * * * * * * * * * *

August 24–September 23

Archangel Metatron uses an energy tool that is shaped from all the Platonic solids, called a *Merkabah* (or "Metatron's Cube"), for healing and clearing away lower energies. For this reason, he works perfectly in tandem with Virgo—the sign associated so strongly with healing (conventional or alternative) and service to others. Wherever Virgo is in your chart is where you can help others.

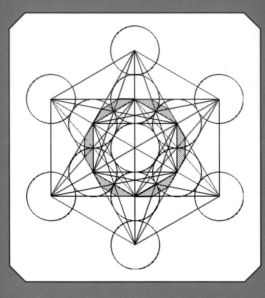

Archangel Metatron's Cube

As you've seen throughout this book, each sign has its strengths and shadow side. Both sides indicate what your life purpose is. Your strengths are to be used to help others, and the shadow side is something for you to personally work on healing.

Let's deal with the shadow side of Virgo first. Those who have a Virgo Sun, Moon, or Rising have reputations for being finicky and negative. To be fair,

Virgos are really good at seeing problems and issues that they refuse to ignore. The good news for you, if you have Virgo in your chart, is that Archangel Metatron takes this energy and turns it into something positive.

Having Virgo Sun, Moon, or Rising in your chart means you're adept at diagnosing, prescribing, and counseling. For example, if someone isn't feeling well, a Virgo will happily offer dietary and lifestyle guidance. Virgos know what's good for others, and so does their archangel, Metatron.

When our energy is unbalanced, Archangel Metatron spins his amazing Cube around our bodies to clear unwanted energy and restore our health. Virgos love everything to be clean, bright, and centered, and the energy of Archangel Metatron's Cube makes it so. It's a perfect fit!

Archangel Metatron is one of only two archangels who were once human prophets—along with Pisces's Archangel Sandalphon. Archangel Metatron was Enoch, the author of *The Book of Enoch*. Now known as the "Scribe of God," he is a teacher of esoteric knowledge. He's the first angel on the Tree of Life in the Kabbalah, which means that he aids people newly traveling the spiritual path. For this reason, Metatron helps children retain their spiritual gifts.

Once again, this energy dovetails with the energy of Virgo. Virgo is an Earth sign, and is all about practicality. Yet the guiding planet of this sign is fleet-footed Mercury, known as the "Messenger of the Gods" and the scribe of the astrological signs. Mercury relates to reading, writing, communicating, and self-expression. If you're trying to understand anything—especially any high-level spiritual concepts—Mercury and Archangel Metatron can help you understand the cosmic mysteries.

No matter what your sign, invoke Archangel Metatron when you're struggling to understand ancient esoteric wisdom. If you're new on the spiritual path and are seeking guidance, ask Archangel Metatron for help. In the same way that Virgo is devoted to helping others, so too does Archangel Metatron help bring about a deepening of one's understanding of life's mystic secrets.

Those who have Virgo as their Sun, Moon, or Rising sign tend to be very cerebral. Although Virgo is a down-to-earth sign, it is guided by the intellectual planet Mercury. This means that Virgos more often live in their heads than their hearts, so they're thinkers instead of feelers.

For this reason, working with the energies of Archangel Metatron is ideal. A part of being on the spiritual path is listening to and trusting one's feelings. Virgos who get in touch with their emotions become very powerful. They combine their ability to intellectualize and analyze with heartfelt wisdom. What an unbeatable combination of thoughts and feelings!

Virgos are often meek and mild mannered, but once they embrace their spiritual and emotional sides, they shine brightly. The more they walk the spiritual path, the more they realize that humility can be balanced with self-confidence. If *you* are struggling with this concept, ask Archangel Metatron for guidance.

Archangel Metatron is also known for his ability to help psychic children and those new to spirituality. Meanwhile, Virgos make some of the best teachers, as they're down-to-earth, wise, and patient. Wherever you have Virgo in your chart is where you can teach and help others.

Virgos are often critical, and skeptical of themselves and others. They also worry a lot due to their extreme perfectionism. Talking with Archangel Metatron when you're feeling either critical, worried, or skeptical can really help. Because he imparts hidden wisdom, he can help you see that worry and criticism don't yield the results you're seeking. Metatron will guide you to be more effective in correcting and improving different situations.

Many Virgos have difficulty handling life here in the three-dimensional realm. Everyone and everything drives them crazy by rattling their sensitive nerves! Luckily, Archangel Metatron is very adept at bypassing the physical laws of the Universe (for example, he can bend time), so he's the perfect angel to call upon if you feel overwhelmed. Virgos want to help everyone and everything, and thereby need to find balance and set boundaries. Ask Archangel Metatron for assistance when you find yourself saying yes to too many favors and obligations.

Sun in Virgo

If you need something done, ask a Virgo for help. This sign goes through life with a fine-tooth comb, analyzing everyone and everything. Nothing is too much trouble for a Virgo. The only problem is that Virgos burden themselves with too many responsibilities. They then moan about their schedules and criticize those who put so much responsibility on their broad Virgo shoulders. They forget that they offered to help in the first place!

Archangel Metatron is great at assisting stressed Virgos. As mentioned above, Metatron has the amazing ability to work with the laws of time. So if you need more time to fulfill all your tasks and duties, talk to this archangel and he'll be more than happy to help.

If you're a Virgo, you'll learn esoteric secrets of the Universe from Archangel Metatron. Many Virgos already know this information intuitively. For example, some have an innate knowledge (without any schooling) of alternative healing, such as working with herbs instead of toxic drugs. Other Virgos are gifted with the ability to use energy healing on themselves, their loved ones, and clients. One of the most wonderful aspects of being a Virgo is an ability *and* willingness to help others. If you're a Virgo and helping and healing others appeals to you, remember that Archangel Metatron supports your work as a healer. He is the angel who's renowned for passing on wisdom from God to humans.

People born with a Virgo Sun are also excellent writers, bookkeepers, accountants, teachers, personal assistants, and researchers. If you're undertaking any of these tasks, invoke Archangel Metatron for motivation and time-management assistance. Being the "Scribe of God," he's there for anyone who needs help with writing, facts, figures, or teaching.

Moon in Virgo

Having the Moon in Virgo is wonderful, because the steadiness of Virgo creates stable moods, while the softness of the Moon energy calms any Virgoan brittleness. Virgo Moon people need life to be methodical and prefer routine; they like their lives to be reliable and predictable.

Virgo Moon individuals are also conscientious and prefer others to be the same, but sometimes their need for everything to be uniform can go overboard. They panic if things are out of place, items are missing, or someone fails to meet a deadline. If you're a Virgo Moon individual with perfectionistic tendencies, try to have compassion for others.

This is also where Archangel Metatron can help. Since he works with time and knows it's malleable, ask him to expand it so everyone feels more comfortable. Also, ask for patience with yourself, others, and the process of life.

If you have a Virgo Moon and have trouble accepting people as they are, turn to Archangel Metatron to assist you in this area. Being on a spiritual path means recognizing that no one is perfect, not even perfectionist Virgos or Virgo Moon people! In fact, if you were perfect, you wouldn't be here in this Earth school at all!

Archangel Metatron will open your mind to esoteric ideas that will help you accept other people and their idiosyncrasies. If you're in an unbalanced relationship that drains a disproportionate amount of time and energy because you're constantly giving (a very Virgo Moon thing to do), ask Metatron to spin his healing Cube around you. Just like a Virgo, Archangel Metatron is here to help!

Mercury in Virgo

Here we have the classic supersmart brainiac. At least, that's the impression you can give off! Of course, your natal horoscope (that is, the astrology chart for the moment you were born) can't raise or lower your IQ. What it does is it gives you *potential*. And when it comes to having Mercury in Virgo, it means you are potential-packed.

Mercury is the planet related to writing, thinking, speaking . . . anything to do with communications. Virgo is the sign that's well known for being modest and chaste and often rather low-key. In many ways, Virgo is the workaday planet. People with a lot of Virgo in their charts can be as sparkly as the next person. But underneath any pizazz, they are all about getting things done properly, working through their to-do lists, and seeing what they can do for others as much as for themselves. And no matter what your actual Star sign is, if you have Mercury in Virgo, you basically think like a Virgo.

There is such a long list of positives associated with this placement: you think clearly, you can sort the wheat from the chaff in any conversation or situation, you're great at analyzing, and you're less prone than many to allowing your ego to get in the way of the facts.

For all that and more—including your reading comprehension and ability to write well—you can thank your Mercury in Virgo. But with Virgo, there is also the issue of self-editing and self-criticizing and worrying about not being good enough. Also, there is a tendency for Virgos to see situations so very clearly that they often become critical or even nitpicky.

The angel guiding your Mercury in Virgo is Metatron. If you have issues with being too self-critical or critical of others, he is your go-to heavenly helper. Archangel Metatron will also help you with your understanding of the esoteric if you ask him. You scored when you chose to incarnate with this astro-combo.

Venus in Virgo

Venus is the planet of love, and Virgo is the planet of modesty. So the fireworks-exploding, hearts, and flowers approach to romance is not for you. Rather, you tend to allow love to grow slowly as you analyze a person and work out if you think he or she will be a good fit for you.

It's not that you are finicky (well, perhaps just a bit). It's rather that you know that the success or failure of your love life depends a lot on whom you choose to be with. If everyone were as practical when it comes to love, there would be far fewer broken hearts!

Venus in Virgo loves to serve, to help others, to make them chicken soup when they're unwell, and to build long-lasting relationships that run on trust and understanding. Your Venus in Virgo means you will take care of your partner emotionally and physically as much as you can. You're all about making sure everyone is okay.

Be careful not to spread yourself too thin with your desire to help all the people you love—there are plenty of people with Virgo Venuses who are exhausted by the effort of ministering to the needs of their partner, ex, child(ren), parents, siblings, neighbors, and so on!

If your love life is lackluster, talk to the angel who guides your Venus, Metatron. He'll show you

there is a lot of beauty in the way you do things. Love yourself and others will follow! And try not to fall for people who do nothing but criticize you! Also, don't be too rigid about the crazy things that love makes you do—love is at least as good for you as bran flakes, and you deserve romance as much as the next person!

When it comes to money matters, your Venus in Virgo means you will rarely overspend. However, remember that being mean to yourself blocks the flow of abundance to you. Ask Archangel Metatron for financial guidance if you need it.

Mars in Virgo

Mars is the sexual-intimacy planet, and Virgo is the sign of the chaste Virgin. So what happens when you put them together? Do you get someone who never gets a chance to embrace his or her sensual side? No!

Virgo might be a chaste sign in public, but behind closed doors, Mars in Virgo can be as sexy as the next person—or even more so! In fact, it's a private astrologers' joke that Virgo energy is the kinkiest. Virgo types (and you are one if you have planets in

Virgo) might come across as modest and chaste. But in an intimate context, they can let their hair down like no one else! Remember, Virgo loves to please, so having the sexy planet Venus in Virgo can make for very considerate lovers. Also, this placement means you're all about being true to yourself, and that's a wonderful thing.

One of the great things about having Mars in Virgo is that although you can drive people mad with your need to analyze the details of any given situation, on the upside you tend not to have a bad temper. In that respect, you're a breath of fresh air for people! Having Mars in Virgo also gives you a big desire to help other people and to be self-reliant. You are wonderful to be around!

Mars is also the planet that helps you get things done. Your Mars in Virgo is very practical. Talk to Archangel Metatron if you are taking on too much. You are goal oriented and organized enough to get more things done before breakfast than most of us will manage in a full day!

Ascendant (Rising Sign) in Virgo

Many Virgo Rising people work as healers. Virgo is one of the most grounded signs, which puts clients at ease during their health challenges. Additionally, Virgos have intuitive access to a wealth of esoteric healing information. The Virgo Rising person can walk through the woods and accurately find plants and berries that are safe to eat, or whip up homemade natural remedies for just about any ailment with a few sprigs from the garden—all of this without having formal training.

This is a perfect fit with amazing Archangel Metatron, who's the keeper of ancient wisdom. So much of what we once knew about Earth's natural healing properties has been lost. Virgo can restore this knowledge, and so can Metatron, who helps humans understand esoteric information, including how to work with energy.

Virgo Rising individuals are experts at paying close attention to detail, and can become flustered when things don't go as expected. If that sounds like you, ask Archangel Metatron to help you relax a little. Remember, this is one archangel who walked upon the earth as a human, and as such, understands many of the challenges that life on Earth can bring. Plus, Metatron can expand time so that you have breathing room in your busy schedule for playing and relaxing.

Virgo Rising people are excellent teachers, as they work with Mercury, the planet of the mind, and make high-minded ideas easy to understand. Just as Virgo Rising individuals often work very well with kids, so too does Archangel Metatron.

Archangel Metatron energy is very focused, as is the energy of someone with a Virgo Rising sign. Virgo Rising individuals have minds like laser beams. Together, they're a formidable force!

✳ ✳ ✳

You can call upon Jophiel for any of the following, no matter what your sign is:

1. For matters related to love

2. To improve your confidence about your appearance

3. To get the flow of abundance moving again

4. When your heart is breaking

5. When you have met someone you want to get to know better

6. When you are about to redecorate your home

7. When you're feeling old and worn-out

8. If you're about to make a big investment in a luxury item

9. If you're an artist working on a big project

10. When your work/life balance has gotten skewed

11. When you want to make your thoughts more beautiful

12. If you're arguing with your loved ones

13. To make your life more colorful and interesting

14. When you're about to enter into a major negotiation, financial or otherwise

15. When you know you're going to need to be diplomatic

16. If you're charged with helping settle an argument between other people

17. To help you release the old

18. When you need to declutter your life or find good feng shui advice

19. To get the motivation to clean your home

20. When you want to release your inner goddess

CHAPTER SEVEN

LIBRA AND ARCHANGEL JOPHIEL

September 24–October 23

Archangel Jophiel is the "Angel of Beauty," so she's the perfect match for Libra—the sign guided by Venus, the planet of love and beauty. Wherever you have Libra in your chart is where you can appreciate beauty, where you can hold beautiful thoughts, and where you can beautify your life.

Venus was personified as the love goddess Aphrodite during ancient times. Libras love beauty, so of course they're paired with the angel who beautifies everything with which she comes into contact.

Both Archangel Jophiel and Libra care about achieving balance. Jophiel helps us restore balance in our thoughts and in our living and working environments. I (Doreen) call Jophiel the "feng shui angel" because this archangel gets rid of everything that's ugly or unwanted, including negative thoughts and energy. Jophiel reminds us that beautiful thoughts attract beautiful experiences, and that negative thoughts attract negativity. If there's a lack of beauty in our thoughts, then our lives will lack beauty—the connection is clear! So when we enter a negative thought spiral, we attract chaos and problems. Often it's a matter of "correcting" our thoughts so that we see someone or something from a different angle. If we ask Archangel Jophiel for assistance, she balances and beautifies our thoughts in order to improve our perspective on life. The more we appreciate beauty, the more we draw it to us.

The beauty-loving sign of Libra represents balance in our lives. As you may know, Libra is represented pictorially in the astrological wheel as a set of scales. Whenever something is uncentered or ugly,

Libra aims to bring it back into balance. Libras are also known as the sign most associated with diplomacy and mediation, because their beautiful way of communicating helps settle differences.

So, if you want to heal a disagreement or misunderstanding, ask Archangel Jophiel to intervene for you. Very soon you'll find common ground!

Libras are also excellent negotiators with respect to setting prices and enacting agreements and win-win solutions. Wherever you have Libra in your chart, you have excellent negotiation skills. And all of the signs have equal access to Archangel Jophiel to bring balance and beauty into their lives.

Archangel Jophiel can also help you beautify yourself. No matter what your sign, if you want to lose weight or change your appearance, talk to Archangel Jophiel. There's nothing superficial about wanting to improve your fitness level, health, or appearance. Fitness can improve your health significantly, and studies show that your appearance can have an effect on your income, promotions at work, and relationships. Archangel Jophiel will gladly help you in these areas when asked. But most of all, she'll help you enhance your beauty from the inside out—inspiring you to smile, radiate joy, and emanate beautiful thoughts and feelings.

Jophiel will guide you to regain balance with respect to eating, drinking, and weight. Think of people who have become obese because something's out of whack in their lives. The part of your chart where you find Libra is where you can rebalance most easily, but we all have the ability to bring balance into *every* area of our lives. Where Archangel Jophiel goes, balance and beauty follow. All you have to do is ask for her help, and because she always says yes, your solutions will soon emerge.

Libra focuses on beautifying the appearance of home and work spaces. Once you call upon Archangel Jophiel, you'll feel an inner pressure or guidance to eliminate the clutter in your home and office. Jophiel will urge you to have a garage sale or donate unused items. She'll then guide you to buy wonderful items to enhance your space. Libra loves the finer things in life, and Archangel Jophiel is the most amazing angel to call upon prior to a shopping excursion. Jophiel will guide you to the best shops that are having sales on the highest-quality items, and she'll even ensure that a wonderful sales associate rings up the purchase!

Although Jophiel will guide you to find these "finer things in life" at the best prices, they still cost money. Fortunately, most Libras are clever businesspeople who know how to earn and spend money well. Libras work hard so they can afford the *objets d'art*, beautiful clothing, and opulent furnishings they want to surround themselves with.

Venus is all about luxury, so it's not surprising that Venus-guided Libras like to spoil themselves and their loved ones. Archangel Jophiel helps with all business endeavors, including feng shui–ing the office to attract more abundance. Just ask Jophiel for her help and she will be there. This archangel's ability to clear out negative energy can help stagnant businesses become profitable.

Archangel Jophiel, like the goddess Venus, is strongly associated with Divine feminine strength. Libra and Jophiel help women make the most of their assets—both beauty and brains. If you have difficulty letting your feminine light shine, then Archangel Jophiel can help you feel comfortable with your female energy, no matter what sign you are.

Sun in Libra

Libra is a Cardinal sign, which means that it's one of the four leaders of astrology—along with Aries, Cancer, and Capricorn. Although Libra is about beauty, this is also a very dynamic sign with the power to make things happen. Similarly, even though Libra's angel, Jophiel, is about beauty and femininity, she's also very powerful. In fact, she's a great archangel to call upon to clear negative energy or shift obstacles, much like the Hindu elephant god, Ganesh. If your sun is in Libra, then you have all this power and more.

Libras are famous for their well-developed sense of beauty, which is one of their strong points. Libra is also a sign that favors women, so occupations involving beautifying or bringing balance to the female gender are excellent for you.

Libras have a strong sense of justice, with their scales balanced in favor of peaceful outcomes. The sign of Libra also guides the law. Archangel Jophiel's ability to move obstacles means that you can defend the underdog and make progress with your power to negotiate, be diplomatic, and restore harmony.

Being guided by Venus, many Libras are artistic. Expressing your creative side will help you release your life force. Anytime you struggle with this area, ask Archangel Jophiel to restore balance. After all, a balanced life encompasses creative expression!

Moon in Libra

The Moon focuses on your needs, and having a Libra Moon means that you require harmony and balance. This extends to all parts of your life. As children, people with Libra Moons gravitate toward having one special friend to keep order and predictability in their friendships. Also, they will teach themselves about nutrition to maintain a balanced diet and act as arbiters of justice on the school playground. As they grow up, Libras maintain strict balance within their adult relationships and diets.

If you have a Libra Moon, you feel it's unacceptable to be out of balance. This is where Archangel Jophiel can help you regain your sense of proportion. She can remind you that you need to take some time to get more rest, or rebalance your diet, for example.

Libra Moon individuals also need to feel that those around them are being treated fairly. This Moon placement endows you with oodles of charm that you can use to help people who are misbehaving. You don't like any kind of discord, so it's really a win-win situation when you manage to get angry people to settle down. Needless to say, Archangel Jophiel will be there for you, if needed.

If Libras become unbalanced, they may display the shadow side of the sign's inability to make a decision. They'll weigh all of their options endlessly and never choose. In contrast, a well-balanced Libra is able to consider one story from various angles. However, this may prevent Libras from forming any opinions or taking a stand. If you do find yourself in this position, it's time to speak to your Moon's Archangel, Jophiel.

Mercury in Libra

Now here comes a fair-minded, eloquent, and silver-tongued sweet-talker! If you have this placement in your chart, you have the ability to talk in a way that often sounds almost like music to other people's ears. And since people like what they hear when you're speaking (or like what they read when you're writing), you have an advantage over most when it comes to getting your own way.

Libra is the charmer of the heavens, and Mercury is the planet that communicates. Put them together and yes, you have someone who is capable of delivering some rather charming communications. This can express itself creatively, professionally, and in everyday life.

Another thing to know about this placement is that Libra is the peacemaker and the negotiator of the skies. So if you often find yourself in the middle of other people's arguments making peace, for example, now you know why! You long for harmony, and sometimes you have to help others work toward it.

Your Mercury in Libra will also stand you in great stead when you have negotiations. You're also very diplomatic and almost certainly have impeccable manners!

The Mercury-in-Libra angel is Jophiel. Should you be prone to that famous Libran indecision, ask for help. Also be careful if you know you have a tendency to flatter people just to get your own way. Manipulation is never pretty!

Archangel Jophiel helps you restore balance and beauty to your life. So anytime you're feeling like you're off-kilter or not seeing life's Divinity, talk to her. Having Mercury in Libra is also very helpful if you work within the legal system. Similarly, if you are upset because you're perceiving injustice, ask Archangel Jophiel to be by your side—she can help with any legal—or just plain unfair—wrangles.

Venus in Libra

You know that two hearts are better than one! In a world where more and more people are stating loudly and proudly that they are happy to be single, chances are that you are not one of them, at least not deep down.

Venus is about love, and Libra is about relationships. Put these two together and you have the classic romantic—the person who is in love with love. You make an amazing partner when you're attached. And when you're single, chances are you're deciding what you want from your next relationship.

Moreover, having Venus in Libra makes you attractive and delightful to be around, thanks to your grace. You are a social being, and you delight in partnership in every form. You make a great friend because you are all about one-on-one relationships.

The Archangel Jophiel guides your Venus. Venus is the planet of beauty, love, and riches. Archangel Jophiel is the angel of beauty. So yes, your life can be filled with beauty!

Is there a downside to this wonderful Venus/Libra astro-combo that Archangel Jophiel can help you with? Well, perhaps you struggle with being a bit superficial at times? Whether you're being impressed by someone else's show of riches or you're showing off yourself, remember that it's what is within that really counts. Plus, you can be a little bit noncommittal in the early stages of a relationship or even fickle as it progresses. Ask Archangel Jophiel for help with your love life and you will receive it.

Financially, you have a very good basis for abundance in your horoscope—Venus in Libra is nothing else if not rolling in the potential to make a lot of cash. Doesn't sound like you? You may need to release fears you have about making money. Of course you can ask Archangel Jophiel for assistance with releasing your inner luxury-loving Libran!

Mars in Libra

You do what you do with the idea of bringing harmony, peace, and comfort to yourself and those around you. Mars is the driving force in anyone's chart. Usually this is a very brash planet, but in the beautified sign of Libra, the rough edges have been knocked off a little.

What drives you is beauty and art, and being creative and artistic. You push for harmony and fairness and things that make the world look prettier.

You're all about getting disputes sorted out with the least amount of anger possible. In fact, if anything, you sometimes don't even want to confront your own anger or anyone else's. That's great, unless you store up your resentment to the point that you end up exploding! You're also strategic and very good at persuading others.

Jophiel is the angel who guides your Mars, and who can help you with any anger issues you have. If you know you need to be more assertive (a common issue for Mars-in-Libra people), then talk to her and ask for help. You will get it. Ditto if you have issues with making decisions or getting things started. Archangel Jophiel can help with this.

Mars is also the sexual-intimacy planet, of course; and in Libra, you can be a beautiful lover indeed. You are driven by the need for things to be nice and clean, though. Don't let any uptightness affect your sexual-intimacy life too much. Let go and embrace the beautiful feelings!

Another thing about having Mars in Libra is that you are likely to do quite well financially, if you want to. Mars is about drive and Libra just loves all the finer things in life, so your drive to go out and earn good money should be high. If you have money issues, of course, talk to Archangel Jophiel.

Ascendant (Rising Sign) in Libra

How beautiful for you if your Rising sign is in Libra! Not only do you have the planet of beauty Venus (associated with Libra) guiding your Ascendant sign (which in turn guides your appearance), but you also have the "Archangel of Beauty" in the same place! This winning combination should help

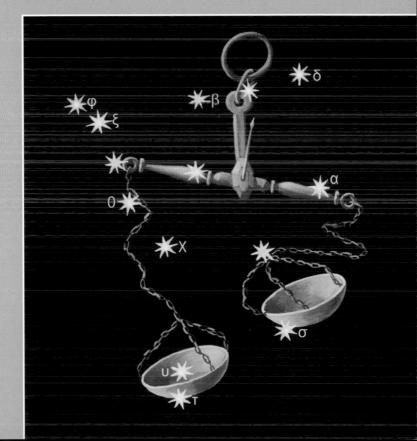

you feel confident that you have a very attractive appearance.

Your Rising sign is the "front door" to your chart. It's the face that you wear, even if it's not always the "real you." No matter what your actual Sun sign is, having Libra as your Rising sign means that in many ways you come across or "present" as a Libra. This is a true blessing, as Libra is the sign associated with a beautiful life. You were born to dazzle!

Libra Rising has substance in addition to all that beauty. After all, Libra represents harmony, diplomacy, and the ability to help people find peace. There's nothing superficial about those qualities.

If you feel shy about letting your grace and charm shine, remember that everyone possesses certain gifts. One of yours is the ability to put others at ease. Ask Archangel Jophiel to help you embrace all of the gifts in your chart, which were presented to you at birth!

* * *

You can call upon Jeremiel for any of the following, no matter what your sign is:

1. If you're feeling scared

2. When you're having to deal with your own or someone else's fear of death

3. If you're wondering whether you've drifted off your proper life path

4. When the dark seems to be taking over the light in your life

5. If you want to connect more deeply with your beloved

6. When you have issues related to your salary and you need the strength to make changes

7. If your credit-card debts are overwhelming you

8. When you fear the repercussions of your behavior

9. If someone has a grudge against you and you want forgiveness

10. When you're finding it hard to forgive someone yourself

11. If you're contemplating doing something against your guidance and morals

12. When you keep looking on the negative side of life

13. When you want to get to know someone beyond superficialities

14. If you have issues around your own or someone else's integrity

15. When you need to keep a secret

16. If you've been through a terrible time and need to bounce back

17. If your feelings are running so deep that they're hurting you

18. When you want to increase your psychic ability

19. When you want to understand yourself better and are prepared to do the emotional work

20. When you're experiencing jealousy issues in a relationship

CHAPTER EIGHT

SCORPIO AND ARCHANGEL JEREMIEL

* * * * * * * * * * * * * * * * *

October 24–November 22

Scorpio guides some of life's most profound topics, such as death, rebirth, and sexual intimacy. It's one of the signs that people either apologize for or brag about! But there's no reason to apologize. We all chose our birth chart perfectly for our life purpose. If you have a lot of Scorpio in your chart, it means that on a soul level you've decided to work with some of the darkest and most misunderstood energies and issues.

Enter Archangel Jeremiel, whose specialties complement those on the Scorpio path. Jeremiel is one of the seven core archangels. His main role is to help newly crossed-over souls review their lives. Jeremiel supports and guides those souls who've recently passed as they review how their actions affected others, and what they learned during their lifetimes.

But you don't have to wait until you've crossed over to have a life review with Jeremiel, as this archangel will assist living people in taking inventory of their lives as well. All you have to do is ask for his help in this regard.

So, Archangel Jeremiel and Scorpio are a perfect pair. Scorpios are among the deepest, and sometimes darkest, individuals around. They're able to deal with a more profound level of life than most people. They make no apologies for facing life's shadows and mysteries head-on. Scorpios and Jeremiel plunge fearlessly into areas that the average person doesn't want to acknowledge. They are truly fearless!

The stronger Scorpio is in your chart (that is, if it's your Sun sign; or maybe your Sun *and* Moon sign; or even your Sun, Moon, and Rising sign), the less afraid you are to be part of the darker side of

life. Scorpios don't really have a casual side, which is something they're proud of.

Archangel Jeremiel reminds us that life has both light and dark sides, and the most important thing is to get an overall picture of how we're doing. Jeremiel helps us clearly look at our current lives so that we can take responsibility for making better choices, if necessary.

Archangel Jeremiel will help you delve into your life review through the process of forgiving yourself and others. This is one of the ways in which Archangel Jeremiel can help Scorpios the most. You may know that Scorpios often hang on to resentment and even engage in revenge. No one can hold a grudge like a Scorpio! The grudge may be justified, but it's only hurting the person who's holding on to it, since old anger is highly toxic.

Each sign has its strengths as well as its ego-based shadows. Yet Scorpios' contrast of light and dark is so strong that it's the only sign to have two separate elements representing it. When Scorpios follow the higher self's path of love and selfless service, they're represented by an Eagle to show that they're flying high with integrity. Eagle Scorpios know how to use their wizardry in service of the Divine. They detach from their own personal desires and trust the

Creator's will to decide outcomes. Eagle Scorpios who have mastered their egos are like living spiritual masters.

In contrast, the Scorpio who wallows in ego energy is represented by the Scorpion who stings others with revenge, dishonesty, and manipulative willfulness. These dark Scorpios use their wizardlike energy to serve their own desires. In addition, dark Scorpios play the role of victims, and continually think that everyone is against them. Lord help you if you get involved with a dark Scorpio!

Most Scorpios are midway between the darkness and the Eagle. If you're a Scorpio who's hanging on to old, toxic anger, consider how free you would feel to let go of those negative thoughts and emotions. You don't have to forgive the action that was inflicted. Forgiveness means that you detox yourself from continually thinking about that painful situation from the past. Forgiveness also balances karma so that you don't have to keep reincarnating with the same souls and situations. Forgiving someone is like stopping the music. The karmic dance is over, and everyone is free to live and love! Ask Archangel Jeremiel to intervene if you're having trouble forgiving someone, or if you want someone to forgive you.

Another trait that may often arise if you're a Scorpio is your secretive, sneaky tendency. This is due to the fact that you hold secrets you feel are justified and that only you can understand. If you have Scorpio as your Sun, Moon, or Rising sign, this sneakiness can disrupt your relationships, cause legal problems, and lower your self-esteem. If you recognize this trait in yourself, ask Archangel Jeremiel to help you. Just because you have Scorpio strong in your chart doesn't mean that you're in any way doomed to play out the negative traits of this sign.

Scorpios often feel misjudged, yet they can be judgmental themselves. They make snap judgments upon meeting a new person. If they don't like this individual, Scorpios won't even acknowledge him or her. Scorpios have the ability to "leave" with their consciousness so they're not really present in the midst of an unpleasant situation.

Similar to the other signs, Scorpio has a lighter and more beautiful side, too. For example, Scorpios are intensely passionate in the best possible way. If they love you as a friend or partner, they will love you to death—unless you cross them, in which case, shield yourself from their vengeful tendencies. Scorpios are very selective about those they spend time with. If they choose you as a friend or lover, you can feel justifiably honored!

There's always a lot going on below the surface with Scorpios, and while that tendency can be a little dark, it's also indicative of their depth. Scorpios are anything but superficial. They are among the most psychic of all the signs, and they feel everything deeply. They won't tell you what they feel or discern, though, as Scorpios seem to be expecting the worst from others if they make themselves vulnerable.

Most Scorpios aren't capable of casual relationships. If they invite you into their lives, you can be sure they really want you there. But they do expect a lot in return, including your riding through life's storms with them. If you're in love with a Scorpio, it's a really intense experience. Scorpios always seem to be at ground zero when drama arises, and some people think Scorpios are drama kings and queens who attract negativity due to their dark outlook on life.

Archangel Jeremiel will help you peel away the layers of the Scorpio onion if you're in a relationship with one. And if you have Scorpio strong in your chart, Jeremiel will help you get in touch with all that is wonderful about yourself.

Scorpios also have an amazingly developed sense of principle. They're as hard on themselves as they are on others. Although they may indulge in sneaky behavior, they expect everyone else to be open and honest. If you're a Scorpio with issues related to integrity, the angelic energy of Jeremiel will help you see your life as it is, and help you review what's positive and also what needs to change.

Sun in Scorpio

Being a Scorpio is an intense earthly experience. While there are certain signs who pretend life's problems don't exist, Scorpios acknowledge and help process these darker subjects. Scorpio is about sexual intimacy, death, and rebirth. Think of the phoenix that rises from the ashes and you have Scorpio. Archangel Jeremiel works with this energy via life reviews that we experience after we cross over to the other side.

Archangel Jeremiel doesn't sugarcoat life reviews to try to make you feel good about where you went wrong in life. Rather, the object is to help you learn. Scorpios do the same when confronting areas that most people would rather sweep under the rug. If you find life too tough to deal with, ask Archangel Jeremiel to help you. Like all archangels, Jeremiel wants you to be peaceful and unafraid. He will gently help you face unpleasant circumstances so that you can learn, grow, and heal.

Scorpios can hold on to hurts and slights longer than needed. If you know that this is one of your issues, then ask Archangel Jeremiel to assist you in opening your heart and forgiving. Sometimes Scorpios seek revenge on those who have hurt them, setting themselves up for negative karma that they could have otherwise avoided. The next time you find yourself veering in this direction, ask Archangel Jeremiel for his help, either silently or aloud. Archangels are there to assist you; however, it's angelic law that they can't intervene without being asked.

Incarnating as a Scorpio means that you're prepared to be a super-intense person who will sometimes feel overcome by your emotions. But it also means that you're ready to connect and engage with life on this level. Archangel Jeremiel steadily accompanies you on this important journey.

Moon in Scorpio

Those born with the Moon in Scorpio tend to be natural psychologists. They have the ability to analyze life and people. This trait means that they have to see every topic through to its conclusion. Think of a sleuth who can't rest until his or her case is solved. That's the way Scorpio Moon people tackle life. They are deep, to the extreme.

Working with wonderful Archangel Jeremiel, you'll learn how to understand your depths. As mentioned, Archangel Jeremiel helps newly crossed-over souls review their lives. He also helps the living take an inventory and adjust their life paths accordingly.

In other words, you don't have to wait until you cross over to the other side to take stock of life. Ask Archangel Jeremiel to help, and then allow yourself some quiet time. If you have a Scorpio Moon, you will find that you need regular alone time anyway. Even if you judge yourself harshly (Scorpio Moon individuals can be very intense with themselves and others), Archangel Jeremiel will help you with forgiveness. The real Scorpio magic happens when you focus your wizardry on love and positive energy.

Because the Moon guides emotion and Scorpio is such a profound sign, those born with this Moon placement tend to have extremely intense emotions. If someone hurts you, you may feel hurt so deeply that it's difficult to release grudges. If you find yourself in this situation, ask Archangel Jeremiel to help you see the person you're judging with loving eyes. Remember, you don't need to forgive someone's actions necessarily. Rather, forgiving is a way of detoxing yourself, regaining your power, and balancing your karma.

Anyone with Scorpio in their Sun, Moon, or Ascendant is highly psychic. Meanwhile, Archangel Jeremiel inspires Divine visions. Working with Jeremiel, Scorpio Moon individuals can learn to trust and highly develop their psychic abilities.

Mercury in Scorpio

Scorpio energy comes out in Mercury in many varied and wonderful ways. On the one hand, Mercury in Scorpio bestows you with the ability to get to the heart of any matter. You might have a frivolous side, but when something is really important to you, you are prepared to dig deeper and deeper until you understand what's going on.

Obsessive? Perhaps, from time to time! In fact, Scorpio is the sign of the detective, so having your mind planet, Mercury, in this sign means you have a bit of the detective in you. Mysteries, spies, the dark side of life, and taboo subjects all appeal to you.

If you find yourself thinking too much about the dark and not enough about the light in your life, talk to the angel guiding your Mercury, Jeremiel. Archangel Jeremiel is not afraid of delving deeply into the darker subjects. Having Mercury in Scorpio means you, too, are good at facing these subjects head-on. However, there is more to Mercury in Scorpio than that.

One of the stellar qualities of this astro-combo is that your mind is sharp like a razor. And so, sometimes, is your tongue! Use your excellent intellectual capacity to its utmost. If you know you're being mentally lazy, have a word with yourself and ask Archangel Jeremiel to help. If you know you have a short temper, call upon Archangel Jeremiel for assistance. Mercury in Scorpio will also increase your psychic ability.

Similarly, Mercury in Scorpio can mean it's harder for you to just forgive and forget than it is for others. But we all need to move on from past hurts and slights. Talking to Archangel Jeremiel when you're having some trouble letting go of the past is crucial. As long as you refuse to forgive the past and make peace with it, you carry it around with you like baggage!

Venus in Scorpio

One of the most attractive things about you is your intensity. Your love is not for the fainthearted! When you have your love planet, Venus, in Scorpio, the depth sign, you feel things through and through, *and you're not afraid to show it!* In fact, Venus in Scorpio can be borderline scary at times—have you noticed? You are not interested in superficial flings or meaningless flirtations, although they might have their place from time to time. But when it comes to really falling in love, you're looking for something that will shake your world (and your body) from the inside out.

One of the major pitfalls to watch out for with Venus in Scorpio is that you don't allow destructive tendencies such as jealousy or paranoia to get in the way of a good relationship. Sometimes your emotions run so deep! This is wonderful news for your partner—if he or she loves you back, you two will

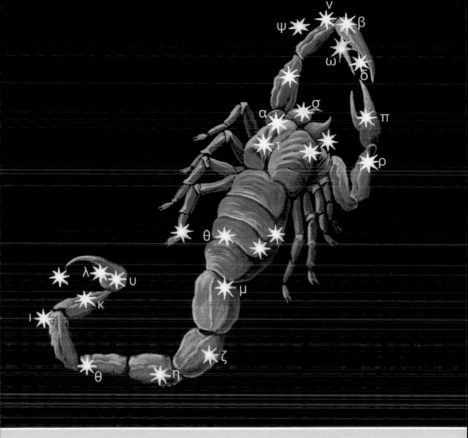

connect from the soul to the body and back again. Scorpios love with their body, mind, and spirit.

However, if you're not living and loving positively, and you're feeling discombobulated as a result; if you think you're addicted to love or to someone in particular; or you have an obsessive crush on someone and you know it's not healthy, talk to the angel who guides your Venus, Jeremiel. He will help you bring things back to an even keel.

Archangel Jeremiel is primarily the one who helps newly crossed-over souls review their lives. So, you may have an interest in the afterlife or mediumship with this placement. Jeremiel can help you take stock of your life and adjust your trajectory while you're alive, too, so ask for help if you feel you have wandered off your path. Archangel Jeremiel also guides you when it to comes to money, so if you have financial issues, ask him to help you review your incomings and outgoings.

Mars in Scorpio

If nothing else, you are a truly formidable opponent in any arena. Mars is the planet of sexual intimacy and drive, competition, and anger. Scorpio is the sign that runs deep, and hangs on for dear life. If you want something badly enough, your Mars in Scorpio will help you chase it long after most of your competitors have given up.

Mars in Scorpio is a very powerful combination, so how should you handle it? For one thing, know your limits and know other people's limits, too. Beating someone, be it in business or in love, can feel like a hollow victory if others suffer as a result of your win. And you're sensitive to other people's reactions to your behavior. So work on yourself if you know you have a bit too much of a win-at-all-costs streak!

Guiding your Mars in Scorpio is Jeremiel, the archangel who is prepared to go where most others fear to tread, into the taboo subjects of sex and death and rebirth. If you have an anger-management problem, it could easily be related to your Mars in Scorpio. Talk to Archangel Jeremiel and believe you can sort it out—you *can!*

The good news is that Mars in Scorpio is very sexy indeed. In fact, some would argue it's the sexiest Mars you can have. Leave that to your lovers to decide. But know that when it comes to lovemaking, astrologically speaking you are blessed in all the right ways.

Mars in Scorpio is a great blessing overall, even if what you have read here sounds almost too intense to be a good thing. *Really*. It's like having a very powerful car. You need to learn how to handle it. Your best option is to work with Archangel Jeremiel. He is

fearless, so nothing you can do or ask or say to him will shock him. And he is there to help you out as you learn to handle the energies in your chart.

Ascendant (Rising Sign) in Scorpio

Your Ascendant sign is the way you appear to others. Since Scorpio Rising people won't talk about their feelings or thoughts without a lot of prompting, you will appear mysterious to others. The Scorpio Rising individual must trust you entirely before they'll reveal their secret inner life to you. In most cases, no one but the Scorpio Rising person is sure what's going on beneath the surface! They can be very mysterious, elusive, and even secretive. For that reason, they're attractive to those who enjoy mysteries and puzzles. If you have Scorpio Rising, you're working with Archangel Jeremiel, who guides Scorpio.

Like the sign of Scorpio, Archangel Jeremiel also works in mysterious ways. Yet if you ask for help, this archangel will assist you in making healthy life changes. When you're trying to understand yourself more deeply, call upon Archangel Jeremiel. He will be there for you at all times, as he is one of the archangels most powerfully associated with your natal chart.

Because of its association with the emotional element of Water, Scorpio is one of the most naturally psychic signs. Of course, everyone has psychic potential. It's just that Scorpio is so open to all energies that they don't filter out psychic input like the other signs. For that reason, Scorpio Rising people make great psychics; you look the part and you have the ability. You just have to overcome your tendency to secretively protect all of the information you receive. Since Jeremiel is one of the archangels associated with clairvoyance and prophetic visions, it's certainly a good idea to call upon him before you do any psychic work. He's there to help you, including telling your clients the information you've received for them.

Scorpio is a sign that loves to go deeper, to the point of becoming addictive or obsessive. If this sounds like you, call upon Archangel Jeremiel to guide you. He will help move you into the fresh air and light, and inspire you to get trustworthy human assistance and support if necessary. Jeremiel can also encourage addicted Scorpio to become humble and vulnerable enough to accept that help.

* * *

You can call upon Raguel for any of the following, no matter what your sign is:

1. When you want nothing more than to go off and see the world

2. When you want to be friendly, but you're feeling shy or otherwise not able to exude happy vibes

3. When you're verging on giving up on chasing your dreams

4. If you need help seeing the lighter side of life or the funny side of a situation

5. When you need something a bit more exotic in your life, and adventure is calling

6. When you're dealing with relationship conflict

7. If you have to teach someone something and you're not a natural teacher

8. To attract healthy friendships

9. If you're obsessing about the details and need to see the bigger picture

10. To help you hear the answers to your prayers

11. When you need to resolve a conflict with someone else or among other people

12. If you need to defuse a tense situation with humor

13. If you're not feeling as generous as you would like to

14. When you're starting a new situation and you need to meet a lot of new people at once

15. When you wish you could be more happy-go-lucky

16. If you have made a mistake in a relationship

17. If you have fallen out with a friend and are not sure how to make up

18. To develop a better relationship with yourself

19. To feel closer to your family

20. To deepen your relationships

CHAPTER NINE

SAGITTARIUS AND ARCHANGEL RAGUEL

★ ★ ★ ★ ★ ★ ★ ★ ★ ★ ★ ★ ★ ★ ★ ★

November 23–December 22

For Sagittarius, life is a game. And for Archangel Raguel, life is a party, because he's the most sociable of all the archangels. His name means "Friend of God," and his focus is on peace and harmony with everyone in the world. This is just like the friendly, easy-to-get-along-with Sagittarian energy.

Like its Centaur symbol, Sagittarius leaps through life with a zest for adventurous, enjoyable experiences. Wherever you have Sagittarius in your chart (Sun, Moon, or Rising) is where you're willing to take risks. It's the part of your chart that's about having fun and chasing good times, without too much thought about the consequences.

Sagittarius leads a charmed life and is associated with the "lucky" planet, Jupiter. Wherever Jupiter goes, good luck follows. Jupiter and Sagittarius are also associated with the ability to "see the big picture." In other words, they can see the whole, rather than getting lost in the details. To understand how useful this is, imagine standing in front of a very large, beautiful painting. Close to the canvas, all you can see are a few strokes and colors. It's only when you take a step back that you can see the entirety of the artwork and appreciate it fully. This is something Archangel Raguel can assist you with. When you're lost in the details, he can help you acquire valuable perspective.

Archangel Raguel also helps resolve disputes, which is perfect, since Sagittarians stay neutral when conflict rages around them. They tend to have a "live and let live" attitude about life. However, if you're a Sagittarian who does find yourself involved

in a conflict, Archangel Raguel is the best angel to call upon. With your famous Sagittarian sense of humor, you rarely stay angry with anyone for very long, especially with the guiding help of Raguel.

Sagittarius is the friendliest sign. There's a warm, familiar energy surrounding anyone who has Sagittarius as their Sun, Moon, or Rising sign. Sagittarians love people, and people love them. They are generous friends, lovers, co-workers, and family members who are even tempered, helpful, and good listeners. What's not to love about a Sagittarius?

This generous Sagittarius energy matches that of Archangel Raguel, focusing on making and healing friendships. As we go through life, we often meet new people we'd like to get to know better. But it's not always easy to reach out to another, because of shyness or fears of rejection.

However, if you're eager to befriend someone, you can ask Archangel Raguel to step in for you. He can open the doors of friendship so that you and your potential new acquaintance can connect. Since Sagittarians are charming in the most sincere way, all you need is for that door to be opened by Raguel, and then others will naturally fall in love with you as a friend . . . or more!

Archangel Raguel is all about harmony, and he can help you find common ground with existing relationships and with new people, too. So, for example, if you're new at a job or a school where you're meeting a lot of people at once, ask Archangel Raguel to smooth your path. Both Raguel and Sagittarius reach out to others with love and warmth. They embrace social situations as fun opportunities to meet new and exciting people.

Being good at making friends is one thing, but being good at keeping them is another. Sagittarians can be so happy-go-lucky that they sometimes fail to notice how super-sensitive others can be. So if you find yourself being a bit "too" Sagittarius, where your shining enthusiasm comes across as insensitive to another person's pain, Archangel Raguel can help your compassionate and nurturing side to glow. In fact, Raguel is renowned for resolving misunderstandings. Of course you need to do your part, too, including apologizing or forgiving where appropriate. But know that Archangel Raguel will be there for you, if you ask, to bring harmony back to any relationship.

So how do you go about asking Archangel Raguel for help? Just utter a few words either silently or aloud. For example, "Archangel Raguel, thank you for restoring peace in my relationship with [name of the other person]."

You can also ask for similar help on behalf of those who are in conflict around you (but not necessarily involving you directly). One of Raguel's talents is to mediate, and to help people see what they have in common rather than what they disagree about. Because Archangel Raguel loves to bring about harmony, he will help anyone of any sign.

Sagittarius always looks on the bright side. People with Sagittarius strong in their chart tend to focus on what's right, instead of what's missing. If you wish you were more like that, ask Archangel Raguel for help. "Looking on the bright side" is a Sagittarian secret of success because thoughts attract reality. Since you will get more of what you concentrate on, ask Archangel Raguel to help you focus on positive things.

Sun in Sagittarius

Sagittarians tend to be very free-spirited, happy individuals who see life's horizons rather than its limitations. What a great blessing! If you were born a Sag, it means that for this lifetime at least, you want to explore the world and its peoples. Sagittarians love to travel. It's one of the reasons why Sagittarius is known as the most broad-minded sign. Of course, seeing the world and discovering new shores is a wonderful way to encounter new friends. Raguel is one of the most gifted archangels when it comes to making new connections. He's all about friendliness and harmony, so it's no wonder that he's the angel to turn to if you want to expand your circle of friends.

One of the few criticisms that people level at Sagittarians (who tend to be very easy to get along with) is that sometimes they talk enthusiastically and endlessly. If you were born a Sag, you're guided by expansive Jupiter, and therefore have a propensity to exaggerate and elaborate. After all, you're a natural-born philosopher who can get on your soapbox at times. This is partly because your razor-sharp mind has so many diverse thoughts and ideas to share with beloved friends.

If you suspect that your fabulous Sagittarius-ness is getting on someone's nerves, ask Archangel Raguel to help you temporarily dial down your enthusiasm to restore harmony in the relationship. Remember that misery loves company, so a depressed friend may not appreciate your comedy routine at that moment.

Reuniting friends is one of Raguel's fortes. And if you feel that a friend (or anyone else) has treated you unfairly, ask Archangel Raguel for assistance. Sagittarius is associated with the law, lawyers, and legal matters, and so is Raguel. You have a mighty ally if you ask this archangel to intervene for you in resolving disputes.

Moon in Sagittarius

The Moon focuses on what you need; and Sagittarius is all about travel, study, adventure, religion, idealism, fun, and risk taking. So if your Moon is in this wonderful sign, then you may feel the desire to take enjoyable, adventurous trips that are spiritually meaningful.

Being an adventurous risk taker can create its own set of challenges, though. If you find yourself in a precarious situation because you've gone off to chase a big dream, ask Archangel Raguel to help you. One of his talents is restoring inner and outer peace to chaotic situations and relationships.

Archangel Raguel excels at creating order where there's chaos. Sagittarius Moon people aren't exactly chaotic, but they can take impulsive action without first researching the exciting new possibility they're suddenly chasing. If you have a Sagittarius Moon and you know that your need for fun sometimes creates havoc, work with Archangel Raguel. He will help you bring order to even the craziest situations.

The Moon is also about your emotions, and it's a great blessing to have Sag here—it means you're unlikely to hold a grudge for a long time, and that's a perfect match for Archangel Raguel, who helps you make and keep friendships. The biggest risk with having Sag so strong in your chart is that you can be a little devil-may-care, which can sometimes get you into trouble. Ask Archangel Raguel to help lead you to friends (and a partner) who will encourage you in your adventures, rather than trying to make you conform.

Mercury in Sagittarius

This combination is a great blessing. Mercury, of course, is the planet of the mind—Mercury is about how you think, write, talk, and communicate with others. And Sagittarius is the lighthearted and happy sign of the heavens. Put these together and you have someone who is able to look on the bright side in nine out of ten situations. And if you know anything about the Law of Attraction—which states that like attracts like—then you know what a great gift this natural optimism is.

That is just one of the possible expressions of Mercury in Sagittarius, but if you have this astro-combo, it's really one of *the* most important. For the record, Mercury in Sagittarius can also be very creative.

The archangel guiding your Mercury is Raguel. Talk to him anytime you feel you're losing your ability to stay positive. It's important not to be hard on yourself when you do fall into a negative thought spiral. Just keep the idea of upbeat thinking in mind.

Mercury in Sagittarius is also wonderful because Sagittarius is all about seeing the whole of the big, wide world. Mercury loves to get away and travel. So this placement gives you an open mind and a cosmopolitan outlook on life.

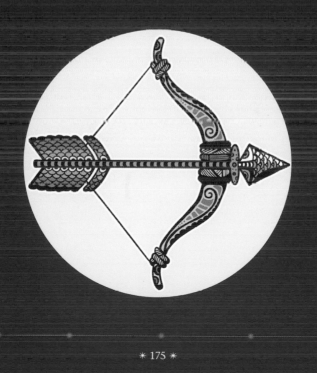

Mercury in Sagittarius means that if you find yourself involved in an upset, you have humor at your disposal—use it to defuse tensions! It assists you when you need to study, and it makes you fun to be around. Sagittarius is one of the most cheerful astrological signs, and your guiding angel, Raguel, is one of the most sociable angels.

What you do need to guard against is talking too much, or those moments when someone might accuse you of being full of a lot of hot air! If ever you feel you're slipping into know-it-all territory, talk to Archangel Raguel and ask him to help you express your marvelous Mercury in Sagittarius in the most positive way possible!

Venus in Sagittarius

For a start, this placement makes you more likely than anyone else to fall in love with a foreigner. Just so you know! But there is more to having Venus in Sagittarius than that, of course. Venus is the planet in your horoscope that is all about love and riches. Sagittarius is the adventurer of the heavens. Put these two energies together, then, and you get someone with a love of travel; who will always be interested in people and places and opportunities from far,

far away; who has a fascination of the exotic; and who doesn't seek to tie his or her lover down.

Having Venus in Sagittarius can also make you rather idealistic when it comes to love. This sounds like a good thing, but it's a double-edged blessing. If you put someone up on a pedestal when you meet him or her, how are you going to react when you realize that like you, he or she is only human?

In addition, you can be overly optimistic when it comes to love. You often assume everything is going to be okay. That's a wonderful attitude, but all relationships need work once the initial honeymoon phase is over. For any romantic issues, you can turn to the angel who guides your Venus, Raguel. Among his many talents, he has a knack for helping end conflicts. If you and your beloved (or your ex) are at odds, Archangel Raguel is there for you.

Also please be aware that sometimes Venus-in-Sagittarius people can be fickle and tend to run away as soon as love gets tough. Talk to Archangel Raguel and ask for help in learning how to stay the course!

Financially, Sagittarius is the sign that loves to take risks. This can make you very rich, if you bet on the right ventures. However, if you know you're a bit too devil-may-care when it comes to money, Archangel Raguel can help you to rein things in a little.

Mars in Sagittarius

What a wonderful Mars you have! Mars is the planet that is all about getting things done, moving forward, and chasing goals. Having your Mars in the forward-looking and energetic sign of Sagittarius gives you firepower.

You should find it easy to be enthusiastic about life, and that gives you a great head start. It's all very well having goals, but you also have the chutzpah needed to really chase them and to make things happen. Moreover, Sagittarius is such a people-friendly

and popular energy. This means you have a way of going after what you want without alienating others. So people are more likely to support you.

There's a downside of having Mars in Sagittarius, but there is always light and shade with every planetary placement. Remember, we choose our charts because we know we need to work on various aspects of ourselves. In the case of someone with Mars in Sagittarius, one problem area can be that you tend toward self-aggrandizement. Watch out for that. Talk to the angel who guides your Mars, Raguel, if you sense you're going too far with someone.

When it comes to sexual relations (because your Mars is also about sexual intimacy), you have a wonderful, no-strings attitude that can be very seductive. However, watch out for being so restless in romance that you end up with a rolling-stone Mars that "gathers" no commitment! Don't give up on relationships at the first sign of trouble. Talk to Archangel Raguel if you need help in this area.

In addition, ask yourself if you are a little too lighthearted with other people's feelings. You're lucky because your Mars means you can glide through life, often not taking things too seriously. However, not everyone is as cavalier as you. You need to consider those meeker mortals around you and their finer sensibilities, at least from time to time!

Ascendant (Rising Sign) in Sagittarius

Those with Sagittarius Rising in their charts are usually popular people. After all, Sag is probably the warmest and most sociable of all the signs. And Sagittarius Rising individuals can walk into a party with a big smile looking for friends—old and new—to have fun with. They simply sparkle, and are irresistible!

Sag Rising people love to talk, but their banter is so harmless that others forgive them for their often-too-lengthy phone calls. In fact, those with Sagittarius Rising are so entertaining that you may find yourself enthralled as you listen to them. If this is your Ascendant sign, you have the unique ability to laugh at yourself and at life, to defuse tension with a joke, and to teach others, formally or informally.

Meanwhile, your strong association with Archangel Raguel guarantees you an appreciative audience for your conversations. On the rare occasions when you struggle to make a new friend, ask Raguel for help. This archangel connects people and brings about cooperation. Raguel will also guide you to take well-planned action steps that fulfill your desire for fun and adventurous learning experiences.

If you know you have a tendency to talk too much about yourself, ask Archangel Raguel to help you balance your conversations. Raguel will show you how to be entertained by listening to *other* people talking.

Sagittarius Rising people also tend to be very playful, refusing to take life or themselves too seriously. Sometimes this may get you into trouble with others who feel you're not according them the respect they deserve. Once again, help is at hand: ask Archangel Raguel to restore harmony and mutual compassion in the relationship.

Your sunny disposition is one of your best assets, so be grateful that you chose this placement. However, if you find that people don't take you seriously enough, ask Archangel Raguel to guide your actions and words so that you're empowered in a lovable way.

✳ ✳ ✳

You can call upon Azrael for any of the following, no matter what your sign is:

1. If you have lost a loved one

2. When someone in your life is suffering

3. When you need to face up to the facts of life and death

4. If you lose your job

5. To heal your heart from grief

6. To overcome fears about death

7. To let go of toxic abandonment patterns

8. To deliver a eulogy

9. When comforting a grief-stricken friend

10. To get reassurance that a loved one in heaven is happy and watching over you

11. When you need to open your heart to love

12. To soften any hard edges in your personality

13. To guide you about how best to memorialize someone

14. If you're feeling older than your years

15. To help you forgive someone who left you

16. If you're cutting yourself off from your real feelings

17. To lose any morbid fascinations with death

18. To stay humble and appreciative of life

19. To connect with your departed loved ones

20. When you want to learn about life after death

CHAPTER TEN

CAPRICORN AND ARCHANGEL AZRAEL

* * * * * * * * * * * * * * * *

December 23–January 20

When Capricorns are children, they exude wisdom usually reserved for older people. In fact, it's said that Capricorns are "born old," and that they acquire a playful, youthful side later in life. Capricorns are extremely hardworking and can be workaholics with unbalanced schedules and job-related stress.

Capricorns also have a near-morbid fascination with death and mortality. Perhaps the reason why they're workaholics is because they know that they have a finite amount of time in this earthly life. Most Capricorns are unafraid of death, though; they merely see it as a phase of the cycle of birth and rebirth.

So it's not surprising that the Archangel Azrael, who helps newly crossed-over souls go to the Light, is Capricorn's primary angel. For those who fear death, the Azrael/Capricorn pairing may sound harsh, but please remember that Capricorn is one of the toughest and strongest signs. Capricorns actually take pride in their ability to handle whatever life (or death) throws at them.

Where Capricorn is in your chart (Sun, Moon, or Rising) is where you're able to stand up for yourself, where you think before you act, and where you learn from your mistakes or pay the price. Anyone who has incarnated this lifetime on Earth with a Sun, Moon, or Rising sign in Capricorn is ready, willing, and able to learn life's toughest lessons. They may not have tough lives, necessarily, but they're realists who see life as it is. For this reason, Capricorns can appear cynical, sarcastic, or jaded. As they become more spiritually minded and connect with their inner

child later in life, Capricorns release their hardness and become peaceful and philosophical.

Archangel Azrael gently heals grief-stricken hearts. Capricorns tend to have lives where a lot of karma is being balanced. So they may find interactions with others tough because they're dealing with people who hurt them or whom *they* hurt in previous lives. The karmic test is whether Capricorns can forgive and release old pain and anguish. Archangel Azrael is very adept at healing the heart in those who have lost someone or something.

Archangel Azrael specializes in helping those who are grieving come to terms with the loss of loved ones. If you know people who are going through situations such as these, call upon Archangel Azrael to heal and comfort them. Similarly, if you need to comfort a grieving friend, or say a eulogy, Azrael can guide your words and actions.

Archangel Azrael is known as the "Angel of Transition and Change." Capricorns are often highly ambitious, successful people; but they can be inflexible, rigid, and resistant to change. Being guided by Saturn the Rock, they can sometimes dig in their heels and get stuck. Archangel Azrael's ability to help people move through life's transitions is useful to Capricorns.

Sometimes Capricorns are so eager to climb life's highest mountains (after all, their symbol is a Mountain Goat) that they overtake and push aside those on their path. Of course, all signs are capable of great ambition, but Capricorns have ambition with a capital A. And sometimes, as a result, they hurt others, who can feel used by them. So Azrael is the archangel to call upon for help if you ever find that an ambitious person has climbed over you. Azrael can help you deal with any kind of grief, including loss resulting from misunderstandings, arguments, and breakups.

Although Archangel Azrael deals with life's toughest issues, such as death and loss, his energy isn't tough at all. In fact, he's comforting and gentle.

When Azrael visits, you can feel his sweet, caring compassion, which Capricorns can benefit from incorporating into their lives. In fact, smart Capricorns realize that kindness and consideration will help them with their ambitions, as business and personal relationships are keys to success.

Capricorns are often very proud of how tough they are. They exclaim, "I can take it!" Archangel Azrael, on the other hand, can be very heart-opening. If you know you're a tough nut to crack and you'd like to get in touch with your softer side, ask Azrael to teach you how to adopt the winning combination of gentleness and strength.

Archangel Azrael is also very useful to Capricorns because he's so "heart based." Capricorn is an Earth sign, but even so, Capricorns can stay very much in their heads. They are so down-to-earth that they're almost *too* grounded at times. That's how they're born, anyway. Capricorns are said to get younger at heart as they grow older. Perhaps they're learning some of the important lessons Archangel Azrael has to offer about living emotionally rather than just rationally and logically. Wherever you have Capricorn in your chart is where you can benefit from functioning more from your heart center.

One of Capricorns' best traits is their inherent wisdom, which probably stems from their capacity to be realistic. With hard facts comes wisdom! Archangel Azrael is also a wise angel. In addition, the grieving individuals whom he comforts ultimately gain wisdom from their grief. Every loss teaches important life lessons if you're open to finding the blessing within a painful experience.

Sun in Capricorn

Being a Capricorn means being older and wiser than your years, until you pass middle age and shed the rigid structures you've built around yourself. Life begins for you when you decide to have fun. Capricorns are a very wise sign (your guiding planet, Saturn, is all about wisdom), and perhaps this "getting younger as you get older" characteristic is related to that wisdom. As you age, you realize that what really matter are love, friends, and family, instead of material wealth and success. Archangel Azrael is a very wise angel who will help you through these life changes. Interestingly enough, if you become a zany, childlike adult who forgets about responsibilities, Azrael can help you find a middle ground. Just ask.

Archangel Azrael's aura color is vanilla/creamy white, and like ice cream, Azrael is oh-so-smooth. One of the most wonderful things about your archangel is that he has a very distinctive, recognizable energy. If you call upon him and ask for healing and guidance, Azrael will give you very clear signs about the direction you should take. Just remember to be open to the signs.

Being a Capricorn can mean that sometimes you're more intellectual, and cut off from your emotions. Capricorns are undoubtedly the masters and mistresses of the stiff upper lip. Archangel Azrael is a wonderful companion to have on your journey, as he will help you clearly articulate your wants and needs. After all, covering up how you feel might seem like the brave and strong thing to do, but you're only short-changing yourself and your loved ones. They would be available to help you if they knew you needed assistance. And as you allow yourself to be real and vulnerable with loved ones, they get to know the *real* you. In that way, you'll be loved for who you are instead of what you do. So ask Archangel Azrael to help you express yourself when you're struggling with life so that the people who love you can help you out.

Moon in Capricorn

The Moon focuses on your emotions, so having the Moon in Capricorn means that you have emotional strength. In fact, people with a Capricorn Moon can be quite tough. They don't feel emotions as deeply as others do. Perhaps their blunted emotional spectrum allows them to better face life's challenges.

That's not to say that all Capricorn Moon individuals are unemotional. A few are actually quite tender, with deep and soft emotional underpinnings. Ever practical, though, Capricorn Moons don't emote over small things that waste energy. But they do hold great sentiment for the things that really matter. Capricorn Moon people won't cry over small things; they save their grief for bigger losses.

Capricorn is guided by Saturn, a planet very focused on timing. Saturn is also considered to be a "cold energy" planet. So, Capricorns can seem cold and even calculating to those who don't understand how deeply emotional they really are. Yes, Capricorn's ambitious mountain-climbing ways can be cold and calculating, but underneath there's a tender heart.

If you have the Moon in Capricorn and have trouble dealing with your emotions, or if your loved ones complain that you're out of touch with your feelings, ask Archangel Azrael for help. He will remind you that you're doing your best by taking on important tasks that might frighten away more sensitive types.

If you have a Capricorn Moon, you may appear formal and uptight. You're not as willing as others to let your hair down and go wild. You're an organized planner who needs structure, and you're also hyper-aware of how your actions today will affect your to-morrows. This is nothing to be ashamed of, so don't let others' opinions sway you. However, if you're guid-ed to lighten up a bit or soften your edges, ask Arch-angel Azrael. He's one of the primary guardian angels looking after you, and he's available to help you.

Mercury in Capricorn

You've heard the phrase "mind like a steel trap." That applies to you, if you have Mercury in Capri-corn. Mercury is the planet of the mind, and Cap-ricorn is the most serious, ambitious, and in some ways, smart sign of the heavens. It's not really fair to say that having Mercury in Capricorn makes you extrasmart. But it does give you the opportunity to develop a more orderly and logical mind, and that alone can make you seem smarter to other people.

Moreover, when it comes to things like study-ing for exams or making professional presentations, having Mercury in Capricorn means you have wit and wisdom, two things very likely to impress oth-ers. Some might wonder how a super-serious ruled-by-Saturn sign like Capricorn could be associated with wit? The answer is that intelligence is often expressed wittily!

The danger, of course, is that you can also be rigid in your thinking. You sometimes look too much at the potential problems, and you can be dry to the point of being parched in your thinking. Don't let that happen!

The issue is that Saturn rules your mind planet, Mercury, and Saturn is the least fun sign in the heavens. So how to do you get the good bits of Mercury in Capricorn while evolving beyond the negatives?

For one thing, you can talk to your guiding angel, Azrael. He is there for you—ask that you get the positive aspects of Capricorn (The logic! The smarts! The ability to concentrate and think oh-so methodically!) without the problematic bits (the tendency to be pessimistic, to lose your imagination, to be inflexible in your thinking and in discussions with others).

You could say that Mercury in Capricorn embodies the idea that with power comes great responsibility. This truly is an awesome placement. Mercury in Capricorn sounds like the mind of someone who could rule the world. Use it wisely!

Venus in Capricorn

Every day, remind yourself there is more than enough love and money in the world to go around! Venus in Capricorn is a wonderful and steady energy. Venus is about love and riches. Venus in Capricorn is the lover who will never let you down, and the businessperson who is serious about his or her ambitions. Venus in Capricorn is reliable personally and professionally. The problem is that sometimes Venus-in-Capricorn people can be so intent on doing the proper, mature thing when it comes to money and love matters that *they forget to have any fun!*

People with Venus in Capricorn are good flirts because they're love-smart. They quickly work out what makes someone's heart tick. But they can also take love so seriously from the get-go that they miss out on some of the lighthearted fun that goes with romance.

If you know you are overly logical when it comes to love, talk to the angel who guides your Venus, Azrael. Also talk to him as your relationship goes through changes, because Archangel Azrael is all about helping humans make transitions in their lives.

Importantly, Archangel Azrael is very heart based. In other words, if your super-sensible Venus in Capricorn needs some softening up; if you know you are too quick to judge your friends and lovers, and you spoil your relationships as a result; if you sometimes fear you will be alone forever; or you feel alone even in a relationship, talk to Archangel Azrael. He will help you make the most of your Venus in Capricorn.

Similarly, if your heart is heavy with grief over lost love, turn to Azrael, the angel whose specialty is healing those who are grieving. Azrael can also help you let go of your morbid focus upon your own death or that of your partner.

Financially, Venus in Capricorn is a big blessing. Venus is about riches, and Capricorn is one of the most serious and ambitious signs of all. Put them together and you get someone who is ready, willing, and able to do his or her best at work and as a result can get to the top of his or her professional tree and do very well financially. Just don't work too hard!

Mars in Capricorn

Mars in Capricorn is the long-distance athlete of the heavens. Mars gives us vim, vigor, and drive. Capricorn is the sign connected to serious planet Saturn, who is all about punctuality, lessons, and strength.

Put Mars in Capricorn in a chart and you have someone who will work slowly and steadily toward his or her goals, not being easily distracted and rarely giving up.

In fact, it's said that when it comes to having Mars in Capricorn, not only do you not give up in the face of opposition, but you actually grow stronger. You keep on keeping on long after your rivals and competitors have given up. If you don't see this in yourself, talk to the angel who guides your Mars, Azrael.

Be aware that Mars in Capricorn is so strong that sometimes you actually need to pull back a bit. Life is not all about competition. If you're on the spiritual path, you should already have a sense that we are all connected. You don't have to beat everyone at everything! Anytime you know you're crossing the fine line into the territory of being ruthless, pull back. This can apply in your personal or professional life. Talk to Archangel Azrael, who can help you with this.

Sexually (since Mars is also the sexual-intimacy planet), you can almost certainly apply the word *stamina* to anyone who has Mars in Capricorn in his or her birth chart. This is a very sexy placement, and not just for men. Capricorn is the sign of the smart businessperson in a power suit; however, it's also one of the sexiest signs. This is partly because it's associated with being smart, and smart can be oh-so-sexy. And partly because you're downright earthy. If you have Mars in Capricorn, Azrael is the angel to talk to if you have sexual-intimacy issues that need sorting out.

Ascendant (Rising Sign) in Capricorn

Having Capricorn Rising is a wonderful blessing. Although Capricorn is guided by one of the sternest planets, Saturn, Capricorns can have a wonderful sense of humor. Puzzling over this irony, many astrologers have deduced that good humor requires brains, and Cap Rising individuals possess this wisdom.

Capricorn Rising people can be blunt and to the point. If you count yourself among them, you usually don't sugarcoat what you say. Remember, Capricorn is focused on being practical and getting to the bottom line. Idle, social chitchat isn't for you! So if you have Capricorn Sun, Moon, or Rising, you say what you mean, and expect others to do the same. You get frustrated with meandering stories or sales pitches that don't immediately get to the point.

This trait dovetails well with Archangel Azrael, who focuses on honesty. However, if you know that your habit of telling the unfiltered truth is hurting your relationships, ask Archangel Azrael to give you diplomacy skills. He can teach you to soften and sweeten your honest remarks so that others can hear you without wincing.

Although Azrael is very powerful and deals with dark subjects, he is not to be feared. He is actually a gentle and peaceful archangel who can defuse emotionally charged situations. Some very good news for Capricorn Rising folk is that any upsets from childhood have toughened you up for adulthood. With this placement, people grow up patient and restrained, and very often will accumulate wealth. Just don't do the "Cappie" thing and try to go it alone when you need help. Remember that Archangel Azrael is around you at all times.

* * *

You can call upon Uriel for any of the following, no matter what your sign is:

1. If you are having computer issues
2. When you are living too much in your head and not enough in your heart
3. If you need an ingenious solution to a problem
4. When you're having an intellectual conversation
5. If you fear progress or change
6. When you are in a business meeting
7. When you are taking a test
8. If you need to think outside the box
9. When you need to make a fast decision
10. When you need to be more practical and grounded
11. When you need more knowledge on a specific subject
12. If you're researching something
13. To understand complicated concepts
14. If you're struggling to keep up with technology
15. For help with your website or assistance with social media
16. If you want to find a partner who understands you
17. To gain confidence when dealing with intellectual people
18. If you want to make stimulating and interesting new friends
19. When you're not sure what step to next take
20. To feel confident about how smart you really are

CHAPTER ELEVEN

AQUARIUS AND ARCHANGEL URIEL

* * * * * * * * * * * * * * * *

January 21–February 19

Uriel is by far the most cerebral of all the archangels, and here he is paired with Aquarius, an Air sign. Air signs, as you might know, are famous for living in their heads rather than their hearts. This is not a criticism, as all the signs have challenges to overcome. Aquarians are famous for being brilliant thinkers and the inventors of astrology. All that time they spend in their heads often leads to inspired ideas and inventions. That's why the two energies of Uriel and Aquarius go so well together.

In some ways, Archangel Uriel is like the wise old uncle who's always teaching those around him. Think of Yoda from *Star Wars,* who wants to pass on all that he knows to the people in his sphere. Similarly, Aquarians are also information sponges. In fact, out of all the signs, they're known as the scientists. Without Aquarius there would be no progress! They take in information, and process it in ways that can change the world. Everything they experience is a lesson.

Aquarians' tendency to live in their heads adds to their intellect. Their ability to detach, and view life dispassionately, makes them cool under pressure, which may be influenced by their cold, intellectual guiding planet, Saturn. Instead of crumbling when life goes awry, they're pragmatic and solution oriented. Because Aquarians are open and expressive, they willingly discuss their trials and lessons and pass along their hard-won wisdom to others.

Where Aquarius falls in your chart (Sun, Moon, or Rising) is where you're able to detach and let others live their own lives. Archangel Uriel brings you personal insights, as well as big ideas. Aquarians are

famous for idealistically relating better to *all* of humanity than they are at relating one-on-one. Similarly, Archangel Uriel is about saving the planet through insights and epiphanies. However, while Aquarians focus more on their humanitarian efforts rather than their personal relationships, Archangel Uriel can do the micro *and* the macro.

Where Aquarius falls in your chart is where you can sometimes be a bit too no-nonsense for your own good. If your Sun, Moon, or Rising is in Aquarius, then you're probably an open-minded idealist. However, in order to enact your ideas for saving the world, you need to enlist the help of others. So, learning to relate to people as individuals with feelings is a part of your spiritual life lesson. After all, Aquarians can become so consumed with their lofty ideas that they come across as aloof, controlling, or impatient. If you need interpersonal relationship coaching, call upon Archangel Uriel for help. As a fellow intellectual balanced with a lovingly open heart, Uriel is a brilliant role model and teacher for you!

If you want a clear example of these energies, think about Mr. Spock from *Star Trek*. He exudes the Aquarian characteristics of a guy whom everyone loves, but who has difficulty processing emotions or feeling compassion for others. Mr. Spock has superb ideas, but what he really wants is an emotional connection. If you find yourself feeling uncomfortable with emotions, ask Archangel Uriel to help you open your heart in a gentle way.

Aquarians are often popular people. However, they seem to collect friends en masse rather than forming tight one-on-one relationships. Emotional intimacy is awkward and intimidating for them, so they avoid it because they're accustomed to being masterful at everything they do. Yet, many Aquarians are obsessed with finding their romantic soul mates! If this sounds like you at all, just ask Archangel Uriel for help with relationships. He is far from being the "Romance Angel"; however, he *is* the wise-uncle angel who can intelligently select a partner for you. Just be sure to follow his lead when he guides you to express emotions, make romantic gestures, and develop listening skills.

Archangel Uriel is the bringer of knowledge, so no matter what your sign, he's the archangel to call upon if you're seeking innovative ideas on any topic. Think of Uriel holding a lantern that illuminates the way. Similarly, if you're feeling lost in life, ask Archangel Uriel to light your path. He will send you Divine guidance through repetitive thoughts, ideas, signs, and insights. If you notice and follow this guidance, Uriel will lead you in wonderful directions.

Aquarians are famous for stating their opinions bluntly, which can lead to friction in relationships. We all want friends who are honest with us, but sometimes the Aquarian honestly is brutal! If you can see yourself in this description, definitely ask Archangel Uriel to help you with diplomacy. He will teach you how to be honest in gentler ways. Uriel is the archangel who's always searching for truth and would love to help you bring it to light.

Aquarius is a sign that focuses on progress and the future. Wherever you have Aquarius in your chart is where you're least likely to get stuck in a rut. However, if you do get mired in a particular life area, ask Archangel Uriel for ideas on how to move forward. He will happily bring you personal insights that make it oh-so-clear which way to proceed.

Sun in Aquarius

Archangel Uriel is very adept at giving prophetic information. Uriel can look into the future, and so can Aquarians, who are gifted visionaries and futurists. Aquarians receive visions of their potential and their ideal paths, and then they become obsessed with helping those visions to manifest.

Aquarians are nonconformists who often don't care about other people's opinions. Also, if your sun sign is Aquarius, you have a talent for forecasting future trends, although you wouldn't follow them just to be hip. So, Aquarians are usually the first people to adopt new styles, often so far in advance that people find their ways (modes of dress, dietary habits, artistic inclinations, and so on) a little bizarre!

Aquarians are the people of the future. They sense where humanity is headed, and try hard to keep the rest of us on the right path.

Moon in Aquarius

Uriel is one of the wisest archangels, so having him as the guide associated with your Moon is a great blessing. Remember that the Moon is about your emotional life, so having this wise sage on hand means you should never be led too far astray emotionally. Indeed, one criticism that could be leveled at those having an Aquarius Moon is that Aquarius can be a very detached and aloof sign, which isn't healthy when it comes to developing close relationships. However, it does help you keep your cool during a crisis. Happily, while you're not overly emotional, you tend to be savvy and wise. If you ever realize you're being guarded emotionally, ask Archangel Uriel to help you get in touch with your feelings. Remember, Archangel Uriel loves to teach, and he will show you the wisdom of listening to and following your emotions.

Your Moon sign reveals what you need, and having an Aquarius Moon means that you must have your space. If you don't get enough alone time, you start to feel tense. When quiet time is in short supply, ask Archangel Uriel for assistance. He's an excellent problem solver who will help you get the privacy you need.

This Moon sign also means you need the space to be as nonconformist as you like. To you, nonconformity makes sense and is also logical. You sometimes have difficulty with others who don't see the world from your point of view. You may argue with them, or even manipulate them into bending to your will. Understand that not everyone has your gift of future visions, or your ability to think freely. Remember to ask Archangel Uriel for assistance in developing compassion and respect for those who may think differently than you do.

Mercury in Aquarius

Now here's a fabulous combination: Mercury is the planet that's all about how you think and communicate, and Aquarius is the sign that's an inventive, witty rule breaker with the capacity for brilliance. And if you think that sounds like a pretty good combination to find in your natal horoscope chart, you are right. Aquarius is arguably the most progressive of all the signs.

You're a forward thinker capable of coming up with ideas that will lead the world toward its next evolution. Okay, so not every person with Mercury in Aquarius will come up with an idea that helps the world turn more modern, but many of you can and will.

Mercury in Aquarius is hungry for original knowledge, and detests the idea of anything tired or routine. You like to work with the facts, which is why this is a winning combination to have. But you can also take an idea and evolve it like few others.

You see what is there, not what you wish was there. You are even prone to flashes of brilliance, and you think outside the box. In fact, it was probably someone with Mercury in Aquarius who *invented* the idea of thinking outside the box. Aquarius is connected to the nonconformist planet of revolution, Uranus; hence, your potential to do things differently.

The downside? Perhaps the biggest potential issue with Mercury in Aquarius is that you can be a little aloof with your fellow humans when you're one-on-one. You can relate to humanity as a whole much better than with one individual—unless you work on yourself, of course. Your guiding angel is Uriel. If you know you tend to overintellectualize when you would be better off living from your heart, talk to him.

In addition, Mercury in Aquarius does sometimes lead people to be very fixed or even conservative in their thinking. If that sounds like you, once again talk to Archangel Uriel. It's a shame to waste your great mind by being too rigid!

Venus in Aquarius

When it comes to love, chances are high that you're *anything except clingy.* In fact, you can probably be downright standoffish at times. Venus is the planet of love, and Aquarius is the sign that says very loudly and clearly "Don't fence me in!" You need space in relationships, and sometimes you act cold as a way of keeping your intimates in their place.

That's all very well, until you hook up with someone who needs lots of attention. You are the sexy, detached person. But if you want to find true love, you will have to stop thinking about it and start feeling it! Once you find it, you can be loyal and devoted to a degree that others find difficult to comprehend.

Uriel is the archangel who guides your love life, if you have Venus in Aquarius. Talk to him if you are finding it difficult to connect on a soul level with the most important people in your life. He is one of the wisest angels of all, so he will help you see where you can make changes.

Make no mistake: having Venus in Aquarius is a great blessing. How wonderful not to need to cling to people. You embrace the idea of *If you love someone,*

set them free. But you have to be careful not to be so laissez-faire in love that you end up laissez-faire-ing your way to losing your lover! Many people *need* to be needed. Having said that, Venus in Aquarius means you are probably attracted to people who are unconventional. May you meet your match! Open your heart and see what happens.

When it comes to money, you will do best if you look at unusual ways to earn your living. Venus-in-Aquarius types are often very well suited to working for themselves, partly because they are such independent types and partly because they don't enjoy living by anyone else's rules.

Mars in Aquarius

Want to talk about sexual liberation? Talk about Mars in Aquarius, then! Mars is the planet of sexual intimacy and drive, and Aquarius is the sign that's all about evolution and getting modern. People born with Mars in Aquarius are often very forward-thinking when it comes to sexual intimacy. Does that sound like you? If not, perhaps you have yet to unleash your inner Mars-in-Aquarius potential.

Mars in Aquarius makes for a willful and independent maverick-eccentric.

Aquarius is the sign that likes to break the rules and isn't afraid of doing things differently. If you have Mars in Aquarius, chances are that you like to experiment and be creative in the bedroom.

The Mars-in-Aquarius person is the lover who wants to be free. That doesn't mean you won't commit eventually; however, the more anyone tries to get you down the aisle and into a house with 2.5 kids, a picket fence, and a 9-to-5 job, the more you are likely to rebel. Heck, deep down you're an impulsive revolutionary.

Suffice it to say that one of the issues that can come up for you is that you end up being a bit of a rolling stone, gathering less moss than you might like. Once you get past youth, you need to find a balance between your need to be your own person and your need to be in a relationship.

Obviously a lot of how your love life pans out depends on whom you choose to be involved with. The angel guiding your Mars in Aquarius is Uriel, the archangel who is a great problem solver. If your intimate life is bothering you or not delivering all that you know it could, talk to him.

Ascendant (Rising Sign) in Aquarius

Remember that Aquarius is also known as "A*quee-rius*" (coined by astrologer Eric Francis). This is the unconventional sign that charts a course without regard for other people's opinions or feelings. Your Ascendant reflects the way in which you appear to others, so if you're Aquarius Rising, you appear to be a rebel or an independent thinker.

Your Rising Sign is the first impression you make. With Aquarius Rising and Archangel Uriel ruling this sign, you may come across as unusual and wise, like a mad professor. Yet, Aquarians take pride in being odd and eccentric, and calling them "normal" would be insulting.

Aquarius Rising individuals make fun friends because they love to walk on the wild side and experiment with unusual activities. That may include drug experimentation, which can be a dangerous path for these carefree individuals.

For example, an Aquarius Rising woman named Jane was a marketer for a massive communications company, but she'd never found it easy to comply with the rigid expectations of the corporate world. As she grew older, her forward-thinking Aquarius Rising side appeared as she turned vegan two decades before it was fashionable. She also got weird and wacky haircuts that tested her conservative boss's patience. Then Jane started meditating and quit her highly paid job to become a meditation teacher. Because her Aquarius Rising allows her to walk her talk so well, she eventually returned to the corporate world, where she's teaching meditation and receiving a hefty salary. People see that she's a little different, and they celebrate that.

So, if you need help embracing your unusual nature, ask Archangel Uriel for help in accepting and appreciating your unique gifts.

* * *

You can call upon Sandalphon for any of the following, no matter what your sign is:

1. When you need some peace

2. If you want to develop your psychic abilities

3. When you want a stronger connection to the Divine

4. To heal through music

5. To be open to creativity

6. When you want to know that your prayers have made it to heaven

7. If you want to work in the music industry

8. When you need to be softer and gentler with someone

9. When you want someone to be softer and gentler with you

10. When you want to write poetry

11. To pray for your unborn baby

12. When you want to sense your connection to all life everywhere

13. To send healing energy or prayers to your brother

14. When you want to better hear divine guidance and inspiration

15. To learn how to play a musical instrument

16. To improve your singing voice

17. To gain confidence with your creativity

18. To help you with the success of a creative project

19. If you want to learn to meditate or deepen your meditation practice

20. If you get stuck on the spiritual path

CHAPTER TWELVE

PISCES AND ARCHANGEL SANDALPHON

* * * * * * * * * * * * * * * * * * * *

February 20–March 20

When you think of Pisces, you think of the water; and when you think of Archangel Sandalphon, you think of peace. And yes, these two go very well together! Pisces is the last sign in astrology, but by no means the least.

Pisces is considered the most psychic sign, one that is connected to the Divine. In the wheel of life, which the astrological circle represents, Pisces would be the senior citizen about to return home to Heaven. The Pisces archangel, Sandalphon, is the one who delivers prayers to Heaven. Pisces is connected to the mysterious 12th House of the astrological wheel, which is a portal to the mysterious secrets of the Divine. It's as though this part of the chart is where Archangel Sandalphon goes as he slips between this world and that of the Creator.

Pisces is also the sign associated with music and film, which aligns beautifully with Archangel Sandalphon, who is often called the "Angel of Music." In fact, Archangel Sandalphon often delivers messages through songs heard in the mind or on the radio. He's around at those times when you hear just the song you need to.

In addition, Sandalphon's energies are soft and gentle, like Pisces. His messages to you come as faint whispers that are easy to miss if you're not listening carefully. If you're talking to Sandalphon and asking for help, stay attuned to meaningful songs. The lyrics could contain the angelic message that Sandalphon wants you to hear.

The strong Pisces connection with the Divine is one of the most wonderful aspects of this sign. The Pisces individual views life on Earth as a beautiful

gift. Anyone who's ever appreciated a gorgeous sunset, the joyous birth of a child, a wonderful meal, or the love of a pet will agree that planet Earth offers special and unique rewards. However, for many people, it's when we adopt a spiritual path that life becomes blissful. Pisces is the part of our chart where we can connect with the infinite Oneness of the Universe. In Pisces, the final sign in the wheel of life, we realize that we're all connected to each other.

If you feel spiritually or emotionally blocked, then ask Archangel Sandalphon to help you reconnect. Pisces is the sign of the spiritual seeker, and Sandalphon is a master at helping people find inner peace. The two go hand in hand.

Pisces is a strong Water sign, which is the element representing emotions and the unconscious. So you can also work with water to uplift and clear yourself. For example, take a dip in the ocean, stroll near a river, take a shower, or soak in a bath filled with sea salts and essential oils. When you set the intention of connecting with water's magical healing energy, you'll be invoking both Pisces and Archangel Sandalphon. How interesting that Sandalphon's aura color is turquoise, which is the color of water! Pisces is a peaceful sign, and being near water will summon relaxing energies into your life, as well as the peaceful angel, Sandalphon.

Pisces is also the sign of creativity and imagination, so Pisces individuals can live in their own make-believe worlds and are sometimes accused of being delusional or even deceptive. Working with Archangel Sandalphon can help people of this sign be grounded and realistic, and also help with communication issues in relationships.

Drawn to otherworldly beauty, a Pisces loves anything sparkly, opalescent, rainbow colored, and reminiscent of Heaven . . . and tends to find meaning and signs in *everything!* Think of the most beautiful music you've ever heard—there's something very Piscean about that music, and Archangel Sandalphon is woven into it!

Pisces individuals are imaginative to the point that they refuse to face the harsh realities of life. Don't expect a Pisces to engage in discussions about problems. On the one hand, optimism and faith are often rewarded. However, avoiding the facts is never a good idea either. Archangel Sandalphon can help with putting dreams and ideals into action.

The energy of Pisces can be so free-flowing that it loses its sense of purpose and direction. It can feel like you're drifting aimlessly in the part of your chart guided by Pisces. A big danger with a strong Pisces influence in your chart is the risk of turning to drugs or alcohol if life disappoints you. Obviously, intoxicants only make matters worse!

Now that you know Archangel Sandalphon is with you, you can turn to him for support. He will help lift your spirits so that you remember who you really are: a beloved and powerful child of God who shines brightly with healing energy and much-needed talents. And if you pray, Archangel Sandalphon will take your prayers directly to Heaven!

Pisces have lofty, exciting dreams, and the trick is to put them into action—otherwise, Pisces becomes stuck in an illusion that they're pursuing their dreams when they really aren't. Also, Pisces tend to have a feast-or-famine relationship with money. They either manifest an extreme lack or a massive abundance of financial flow. This is partly because action is needed for dreams to become viable in the marketplace. If Pisces only dreams about their potential, there's no way to attract an income. This lack of action sometimes stems from overindulging in intoxicants. But a sober and focused Pisces who puts dreams into action is unstoppable in many ways, including financially.

Sun in Pisces

Like the Archangel Sandalphon, if you're a Piscean Sun individual, you bring peace wherever you go. You have inner peace, and you also exude it outwardly. You won't compromise yourself with a meaningless job or boring relationship. You're focused on dramatic dreams that light up your soul. You also have the ability to help others realize their dreams and life purpose. You're a seeker of the highest order and easily connect with Archangel Sandalphon, the mystical angel whose primary role is to carry humans' prayers to God.

Pisces is the final sign of the astrological wheel, and remarkably psychic. Perhaps those born under this sign have incarnated through all 11 others and have fully developed their human potential. If you're interested in deepening your connection to Spirit, call upon Archangel Sandalphon, the angel of your Sun sign.

Like Pisces, Archangel Sandalphon is strongly associated with music. Pisces individuals excel in music-related activities, poetry, film, and the arts in general. When you ask Archangel Sandalphon for help, the answer will often come to you through a song that you "happen" to hear.

To put your dreams into motion and achieve the career and blissful life you seek, ask Archangel Sandalphon to help you with motivation, focus, and organization. Unlike the younger signs, you aren't materially ambitious or competitive. But you are idealistic and desire a better life for yourself and others.

Moon in Pisces

If people born with a Pisces Sun are naturally psychic, this goes double for those born with a Pisces Moon. In fact, if your Moon is in Pisces, you're deeply tuned in to the cosmos. You know what people are thinking, and you understand the Universe's secrets about energy. It's very important for those born with this placement to learn how to deal with the cosmic information they receive on a regular basis. To learn the practical applications of your esoteric knowledge, turn to Archangel Sandalphon. He will help you experience the heights of joy by putting your spiritual wisdom into action.

Unfortunately, there are many Pisces Moon people who dislike their extreme sensitivity, so they retreat into isolation or intoxication, as those who incarnate with a Pisces Moon have addictive tendencies. Pisces is the sign that is very close to the Divine, and sometimes the human reaction to getting so close to Source is "overwhelm-ment." As a result, drugs and alcohol can cause issues for those born under this sign.

But please don't deprive others of your gifts of sensitivity—you are needed in this world! Talk to Archangel Sandalphon if you're abusing substances or isolating yourself. Sandalphon can guide you to a trustworthy counselor or a free support group. Remember that intoxicants rob you of creative ideas and the energy you need to turn your dreams into reality.

A Pisces Moon individual named Robert was a classic example of someone who'd allowed his love of "altered states" to get out of hand. In his youth, he traveled to India, found a guru, and tried to fulfill his Pisces Moon needs by chanting and dancing all night, sober and happy. However, once he left the ashram to return to his suburban life, he started to use drugs and alcohol as a replacement. It would have been far better to channel this spiritual lunar placement into healthier Pisces Moon tendencies such as daydreaming, working with nighttime dreams, meditating, creating or enjoying music, and bringing a gentle magic into the lives of those around him.

The Moon tells you what you need and what "feeds" you. If your Moon is in Pisces, you need poetry, romance, and beautiful experiences in your life. Ask Archangel Sandalphon for help in creating your dream world.

Mercury in Pisces

Having Mercury in Pisces is a wonderful thing. Mercury-in-Pisces people tend to speak softly and gently. Mercury is the planet of communications, associated with the way you think and write and speak. Pisces is the sign of music, poetry, and dreams. Put all these together and your voice and words can be as beautiful as a song.

On top of that, you listen well, too. Pisces is a very gentle sign. Very *un*pushy. As a result, people with Mercury in Pisces tend to be not too pushy themselves—and that can come as a welcome relief to the rest of us, as we deal with the *Look at me!* culture of the 21st century!

The archangel ruling your Mercury is Sandalphon, a very harmonious angel. So here you have your mind planet, Mercury, ruled by a planet with this lovely soft energy. Yes, it's a lovely combination for those who deal with you!

Do be aware that Mercury in Pisces can be a little bit scattered. Mercury-in-Pisces people are more intuitive than they are logical. And while that is also a beautiful thing, there is no doubt that sometimes they can get a bit lost when it comes to modern inventions like spreadsheets or working with cold, hard facts and figures. Do talk to Archangel Sandalphon when you have trouble getting organized.

Don't for one second fear that you're in any way less than anyone else because of having this placement. Actually, Pisces is the sign of the visionary and the dreamer—you can dream bigger dreams than most, and with Archangel Sandalphon's help, you can make them real.

This placement of Mercury in Pisces is also wonderful for enhancing your innate psychic ability. If this is something you would like to develop, talk to Archangel Sandalphon. He will also help you do dream work, whether you want to analyze your dreams for better self-understanding or follow the guidance from your dreams.

Venus in Pisces

This is the placement of romantics, poets, and dreamers. Venus in Pisces means you can romance your beloved to the ends of the earth, read him or her sonnets in bed, talk about his or her dreams, and help him or her see life through rose-colored glasses. *Sigh.*

However, there is a *but.* When it comes to love, you can be a bit of a slippery fish! For one thing, you're unutterably idealistic in love. Sometimes, people with Venus in Pisces are let down because they put their partners on a pedestal and are shocked when the person they idolized turns out to have real-life faults and flaws like anyone else!

For an astrologer, seeing Venus in Pisces on someone's horoscope birth chart is like seeing a little love bug standing there with his or her heart wide open, waiting for true love to come find him or her. Sometimes such people get hurt easily, because not everyone has the same romantic inclinations. Sometimes they get very confused by love, because Pisces doesn't always see things clearly. And sometimes they meet the soul mate they always knew they would find, and they live and love happily ever after.

And how are you meant to make sure you fall in the third group? You need to be smart about whom you get involved with. Trust your instincts, and take extra care to avoid people with anything even resembling substance-abuse issues. Run the other way if they drink too much or rely upon legal or street drugs to sleep or relax. Your angels will give you red-flag warnings, and it's essential that you step outside of your fairy-tale love bubble to see and follow these angelic warning signs!

The angel guiding your love life is Sandalphon, the archangel of music who helps your artistic and romantic side be down-to-earth. Talk to him when difficult situations develop. Ask him to help you see your partners more clearly.

Also ask Archangel Sandalphon to help you with money matters. Venus rules your riches, and having Venus in Pisces can mean that you earn your money in inspirational ways. But it can also mean you are not quite logical enough when it comes to dealing with cold, hard cash! Archangel Sandalphon can help you with that. In fact, he wants to help you in any way he can! Think of Sandalphon as your inner artist's manager!

Mars in Pisces

With Mars in Pisces, you can tread the way of the peaceful warrior. Mars is the planet of assertion, but Pisces is the last sign to push itself forward. You need to understand this and work on this.

If you have Mars in Pisces, you have superpowers of intuition, so use them constantly, in business and when it comes to your personal life. Even if you don't want to sideline your competition, you can at least stay one step ahead by *tuning in psychically* to what is going on around you.

Mars is the planet that helps you move toward success, and having Mars in Pisces means success for you is tied to using your intuitive gifts. Got the message? The greater your sense of connection to Spirit, the more successful you can be.

Overall, you are probably more of a lover than a fighter. Of course, we all have some fight in us, but with this astro-combo, you are more inclined to fight someone by biding your time, or by confusing your opponent. (Hey, neat tactic, by the way!)

The negative is that you can be a little afraid of confrontation and therefore end up not getting what you want. Plus, when you do get angry, you often end up feeling quite guilty about it.

If you recognize yourself in this at all, talk to the angel who guides your Mars, Sandalphon.

Sexually (since Mars also rules sexual intimacy), Mars in Pisces is steeped in romance as much as it is in lust. You tend to go with the flow when it comes to making romantic sexual connections, rather than chasing after people. That's fine, but remember the words of the ancient Greek writer Sophocles: "Fortune is not on the side of the fainthearted!" Go after your goals! Again, if you have trouble with this, talk to Archangel Sandalphon, who is ready, willing, and able to help you.

Ascendant (Rising Sign) in Pisces

Your Rising Sign indicates how other people see you. Pisces Rising means that people view you as a gentle and easygoing person (even if you're really not). You are not your Rising Sign; it's just the way that others perceive you. However, some may misjudge you as being a pushover and try to take advantage of your sweet Pisces Rising nature. But they'll soon discover that the true you is much tougher than you appear on the outside.

The classic Pisces Rising person will have no trouble connecting with Archangel Sandalphon or any other angel. In fact, while everyone else is trying to understand what all of this means, the Pisces Rising individual will have already created a meditation altar with pictures of supportive archangels. Someone with Pisces Rising will already be communicating with his or her angels. Pisces is a very spiritual sign, and to have Pisces Rising means being comfortable with one's spirituality.

If you're already on the spiritual path and you get stuck, remember to ask Archangel Sandalphon for assistance. He is there for you in every way, including taking your prayers up to Heaven so that they may be answered.

✳ ✳ ✳

AFTERWORD

We sincerely hope that you've enjoyed learning about the archangels in your chart. Delving into astrology can be a passing phase, or it can become a lifelong interest. The more you understand your chart, the more you can understand yourself. It's uncanny, the way it works.

And by discovering more about your loved ones' charts, you'll also start to understand *them* better. Astrology, like the angels, is a guide that is always there to support you if you remember to use it for the good of yourself and others.

Doreen and Yasmin

* * *

ABOUT THE AUTHORS

Doreen Virtue holds B.A., M.A., and Ph.D. degrees in counseling psychology. She has written about astrology in her book *The Care & Feeding of Indigo Children*, and in a number of magazine columns.

Doreen has appeared on *Oprah, CNN, The View,* and other television and radio programs, and she writes regular columns for *Woman's World* magazine. Her products are available in most languages worldwide, on Kindle and other eBook platforms, and as iTunes apps. For more information on Doreen and the workshops she presents, please visit: www.AngelTherapy.com.

You can listen to Doreen's live weekly radio show, and call her for a reading, by visiting: HayHouseRadio.com®.

ANGEL THERAPY®

*

Yasmin Boland is one of most prolific astrology writers in the world, read by millions of people each week via her columns in magazines, newspapers, and on websites. She's also the author of two novels, one work of nonfiction, plus two series of astrology books. She's been published in Australia, Canada, India, Portugal, and the U.K. Yasmin's heritage stems from the mystical islands of Malta and Ireland. To learn more about Yasmin or to have your astrological chart done, please visit: www.yasminboland.com/ AngelCharts.

* * *

NOTES

NOTES

HAY HOUSE TITLES OF RELATED INTEREST

YOU CAN HEAL YOUR LIFE, the movie, starring
Louise L. Hay & Friends (available as a 1-DVD
program and an expanded 2-DVD/set)
Watch the trailer at: www.LouiseHayMovie.com

THE SHIFT, the movie, starring Dr. Wayne W. Dyer
(available as a 1-DVD program and an expanded
2-DVD set) Watch the trailer at: www.DyerMovie.com

✳

*CELEBRATING THE UNIVERSE!: The Spirituality
and Science of Stargazing,* by James Mullaney

I CAN SEE CLEARLY NOW, by Dr. Wayne W. Dyer

*THE NUMEROLOGY GUIDEBOOK: Uncover Your Destiny
and the Blueprint of Your Life,* by Michelle Buchanan

TUNE IN: Follow Your Intuition from Fear to Flow,
by Sonia Choquette

*THE TURNING POINT: Creating Resilience in
a Time of Extremes,* by Gregg Braden

*YOUR HIDDEN SYMMETRY: How Your Birth Date
Reveals the Plan for Your Life,* by Jean Haner

All of the above are available at your local bookstore,
or may be ordered by contacting Hay House (see next page).

We hope you enjoyed this Hay House Lifestyles book. If you'd like to receive our online catalog featuring additional information on Hay House books and products, or if you'd like to find out more about the Hay Foundation, please contact:

Hay House, Inc.
P.O. Box 5100,
Carlsbad, CA 92018-5100

(760) 431-7695 or (800) 654-5126
(760) 431-6948 (fax) or (800) 650-5115 (fax)
www.hayhouse.com® • www.hayfoundation.org

✳

Published and distributed in Australia by: Hay House Australia Pty. Ltd., 18/36 Ralph St., Alexandria NSW 2015 • *Phone:* 612-9669-4299 • *Fax:* 612-9669-4144 • www.hayhouse.com.au

Published and distributed in the United Kingdom by:
Hay House UK, Ltd., Astley House, 33 Notting Hill Gate, London W11 3JQ • *Phone:* 44-20-3675-2450
Fax: 44-20-3675-2451 • www.hayhouse.co.uk

Published and distributed in the Republic of South Africa by: Hay House SA (Pty), Ltd., P.O. Box 990, Witkoppen 2068 *Phone/Fax:* 27-11-467-8904 • www.hayhouse.co.za

Published in India by: Hay House Publishers India, Muskaan Complex, Plot No. 3, B-2, Vasant Kunj, New Delhi 110 070 • *Phone:* 91-11-4176-1620 • *Fax:* 91-11-4176-1630 • www.hayhouse.co.in

Distributed in Canada by: Raincoast Books, 2440 Viking Way, Richmond, B.C. V6V 1N2 • *Phone:* 1-800-663-5714
Fax: 1-800-565-3770 • www.raincoast.com

✳

Take Your Soul on a Vacation

Visit www.HealYourLife.com® to regroup, recharge, and reconnect with your own magnificence.
Featuring blogs, mind-body-spirit news, and life-changing wisdom from Louise Hay and friends.

Visit www.HealYourLife.com today!

Free e-newsletters from Hay House, the Ultimate Resource for Inspiration

Be the first to know about Hay House's dollar deals, free downloads, special offers, affirmation cards, giveaways, contests, and more!

 Get exclusive excerpts from our latest releases and videos from *Hay House Present Moments*.

 Enjoy uplifting personal stories, how-to articles, and healing advice, along with videos and empowering quotes, within *Heal Your Life*.

 Have an inspirational story to tell and a passion for writing? Sharpen your writing skills with insider tips from *Your Writing Life*

Sign Up Now!

Get inspired, educate yourself, get a complimentary gift, and share the wisdom!

http://www.hayhouse.com/newsletters.php

Visit www.hayhouse.com to sign up today!

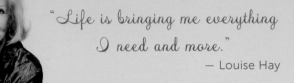